The adventure is beginning

The adventure is beginning

Readings, prayers, poems and actions
for Advent and Christmas

Neil Paynter (ed)

wild goose
publications

www.**ionabooks**.com

Overseas distribution
Australia: Willow Connection Pty Ltd, Unit 4A, 3–9 Kenneth Road,
Manly Vale, NSW 2093
New Zealand: Pleroma, Higginson Street, Otane 4170, Central Hawkes Bay

Printed by Bell & Bain, Thornliebank, Glasgow

FSC
www.fsc.org
MIX
Paper from
responsible sources
FSC® C007785

Contents

Introduction

Someone once said to me that what they appreciate about books like this, and the one before it, *In Love with the Life of Life*, is all the different voices. Reading collections like this, they told me, helped them to feel part of '*a little community of hope*'.

In *The Adventure Is Beginning*, Leader of the Iona Community, Ruth Harvey, writes:

'*The first two verses of Isaiah's prophecy speak of a people beckoning their God, who they know will turn the world upside down. And so we join our voice with the voices of others, welcoming, willing, wooing the arrival of a God who will overturn injustice and will midwife the birth of a new world order …*'

I hope that reading this book helps you to feel part of a community of hope – in 2020-2021 we need hope – and I hope that it challenges you to pray and work for a world turned upside down, for the birth of a new world order. One where we, in the West, learn to live with less and climate change is halted, where refugees and asylum seekers are welcomed and cherished, where poverty is made history …

Thank you so much for all that you do in your community and in the community of the world. We are all sparks of the Light. Let's keep on encouraging and inspiring each other.

To root this book and give writers a discipline, the Bible readings are based on the Revised Common Lectionary, Year B. The Bible readings don't follow the lectionary strictly though: folk were asked to choose a few verses from one reading in the lectionary. While the Bible readings connect to the lectionary for 2020/2021, this book may be used during Advent and Christmas in any year. However if you want to read it in connection with the Revised Common Lectionary, there are four additional daily readings in the Appendix which allow for the book to be used every third year, when the readings fall in Year B.

Reflecting a diverse community of hope, there's a good range of different writing styles here: biblical exegesis, personal reflection, meditations, poetry, prayer …

Thanks so much to everyone who contributed to *The Adventure Is Beginning*. It was a privilege to be entrusted with your writing.

Thanks to writer/editor/friend Ruth Burgess for her ability to get inside lectionaries, and for calmly being there.

'Advent stories tell us: "Get ready!" – for something hugely momentous is about to happen. "Prepare yourself!", because after this nothing will ever be the same again …' (Ruth Harvey)

And so, with Christmas and a New Year just up ahead, let's prepare by saying this beautiful prayer together:

Give us the courage to follow your light
along the road of compassion, of peace, of community,
so that we can become the people you created us to be.
God says: 'Here I am – knocking on your door.'
The door opens – the New Year is ahead – the adventure is beginning.
(Isabel Whyte)

– Neil Paynter, early October, Biggar, Scotland

Readings, prayers,
poems and actions
for Advent and Christmas

First Sunday of Advent

Bible reading:

O that you would tear open the heavens and come down,
*   so that the mountains would quake at your presence –*
*   as when fire kindles brushwood*
*   and the fire causes water to boil –*
to make your name known to your adversaries,
*   so that the nations might tremble at your presence!*

Isaiah 64:1–2 (NRSV)

But let your hand be upon the one at your right hand,
*   the one whom you made strong for yourself.*
Then we will never turn back from you;
*   give us life, and we will call on your name.*

Restore us, O Lord God of hosts;
*   let your face shine, that we may be saved.*

Psalm 80:17–19 (NRSV)

'As long as we live, there is a future for creation,
a future for the universe.

We know this, we know this,
we know God's Kingdom. It will come.'

From 'Malembe'[1]

Advent points us forward to God's future – a future pregnant with the promise of restoration, salvation, new life delivered in the birth of a baby. This promise which we know will come is accompanied, like any birth, by elemental moments powerful enough to make mountains quake, nations tremble and the people of God turn in awe to the One who births us all. The power of the largest entities we can imagine, mountains and nations, is nothing in the presence of the elemental power of God.

Advent stories tell us: 'Get ready!' – for something hugely momentous is about to happen. 'Prepare yourself!', because after this nothing will ever be the same again. Mary, as an expectant mother, would have felt an inkling of this power.

The first two verses of Isaiah's prophecy speak of a people beckoning their God, who they know will turn the world upside down. And so we join our voice with the voices of others, welcoming, willing, wooing the arrival of a God who will overturn injustice and will midwife the birth of a new world order. *'Malembe, Malembe … we know God's Kingdom. It will come.'*

But we don't need to experience childbirth or even an earthquake to be shaken to the core or to be reminded of our task in ushering in God's Kingdom.

Millions of people have their lives shaken daily by the struggle to provide food for a family, the search for a home, the grief of an unexpected or untimely death. Lives are shaken to the core by a violent virus that rips, unseen, through our communities; by a refugee crisis on our borders that is exacerbated by political power games; by the hypocrisy of the powerful who justify the shameless abuse of wealth and over-consumption of the earth's resources.

In response to God's call and promise at Advent and in the face of injustice at all times, we are each called to be equally shaken, enraged, impassioned to act for justice in the name of the elemental Christ whose birth we await. George Fox trembled at the injustice and hypocrisy apparent to him in six-teenth-century England. His shaking with both fury and the power of the Holy Spirit inspired him and others to establish a religious community ded-icated to the transformation of all of society through prayer and peaceful, radical action. His visible 'quaking' in the presence of the law earned him and his followers the nickname 'Quaker'. Perhaps it is part of the Christian charism to be shaken to the core, to quake, to rant and to rage at injustice and to stand in solidarity and in radical, prayerful activism with those who, in the words of the song, *'know God's Kingdom. It will come.'*

Into this time of quaking speaks a steadying voice. The Psalmist reassures us of a powerful presence, as powerful as fire, wind, earth, water, a close companion who will restore us, will save and deliver us. So we wait both tenderly and impatiently for the One who will shake us and our world to the core and who will stay with us through the turmoil. We wait for the One who will restore our hope and faith.

'Malembe', a song from the Democratic Republic of Congo, captures both the awe and the promise of Advent. As long as there is breath in our bodies, as long as we pray, as long as we move and follow Jesus – then there is a future for creation. Our task is to live, to speak, to pray, to follow so that God's Kingdom will come – we know this.

'Malembe, malembe,
malembe tokotambola …

We know this, we know this,
we know God's Kingdom. It will come.

Prayer:

Loving God,
may our waiting in Advent
be pregnant with impatience
for the restoration of relationships
where they are torn or hurting.

May our quaking in your presence
be a sign of our passion
for justice for those
with no home or no hope.

May our trembling on our knees
speak of the energy
that motivates us
to take action for peace.

Living God of delightful waiting,
we thank you
for this time of deep anticipation.

May we live up to our aspirations,
and to your promise
of a glorious Kingdom which will come.
This we pray in the name of Jesus.
Amen

Ruth Harvey

Note:

1. 'Malembe', original words and music copyright © 2012 Joseph Kabemba
   Mwenze, Kinshasa, Democratic Republic of Congo. Translation Carolyn Kap-
   pauf, © Copyright Control. From *The Truth that Sets Us Free: Biblical Songs for
   Worship*, Wild Goose Publications, 2012, John L. Bell, Graham Maule and the
   Wild Goose Resource Group (www.wildgoose.scot)

First Week of Advent, Monday

Bible reading:

They shall beat their swords into ploughshares,
    and their spears into pruning hooks;
nation shall not lift up sword against nation,
    neither shall they learn war any more;
but they shall all sit under their own vines and under their own fig trees,
    and no one shall make them afraid;
    for the mouth of the Lord of hosts has spoken.

Micah 4:3a–4 (NRSV)

Reflection: Nightmares and daydreams

When I was little, God,
my head was full of dreams –
dreams I remembered when I woke;
dreams that disturbed my sleep;
recurring dreams, like that one where I believed
we were going to be invaded by aliens from outer space:
all sorts of weird, colourful craft appearing in the sky,
night after night;
never actually attacking, just hanging there,
but I would wake up terrified.

They weren't all nightmares, though. I had lots of good dreams.
And they didn't all happen in my sleep, either;
I would often dream during the day.
Grown-ups told me I had an overactive imagination.

But I don't know why I'm telling you all this, God:
you know everything that goes on in my head,
and ever did.
In fact, I have wondered whether a few of them

actually came from you in the first place!
That might explain why the same ones
kept coming back ...
And why, sometimes, different people have the same dreams.

There I go again with my overactive imagination!

I know this, though, God:
Most of my favourite people in the Old Testament
were the prophets.
They had amazing dreams –
and wanted everyone to know about them.
And they talked about them as if they really did come from you.

Lots of them were nightmares.
I'm not so keen on those; they disturb my sleep!
I know they came as warnings, telling folk to mend their ways,
but it's when people feel they are under attack
that they start preparing for war.

But there were good dreams, too; inspiring dreams:
like that one Micah had –
about recycling weapons as agricultural tools,
and *not* studying war any more.

And Isaiah.
He had exactly the same dream as Micah, didn't he!*
So that one *must* have come from you!

In fact, despite all the nightmares
that made people wake up so terrified,
and pray that you would come one day and
destroy all their enemies ...

... there were just enough dreamers like Micah and Isaiah,
with their visions of a Kingdom of peace,
to prepare the way for your coming.

And there still are! Just enough!
Didn't Martin Luther King have a dream like that?
Didn't Nelson Mandela? Didn't Mahatma Gandhi?
Don't you give your recurring dream,
your good dream,
to prophets of every age?
And faith?

Prayer:

God of the Prince of Peace,
dream your dream in us,
and give us the imagination and courage
to believe it,
to prepare for it,
to live as if it is already so,
and to try to make good dreams come true.

* *Isaiah 2:1–4*

Brian Woodcock

First Week of Advent, Tuesday

Bible reading:

Pour out your anger on the nations
that do not know you,
and on the kingdoms
that do not call on your name.
For they have devoured Jacob
and laid waste his habitation.

Do not remember against us the iniquities of our ancestors;
let your compassion come speedily to meet us,
for we are brought very low.
Help us, O God of our salvation,
for the glory of your name;
deliver us, and forgive our sins,
for your name's sake.

Psalm 79:6–9 (NRSV)

Reflection:

Revenge? Really? Is this what we want in Advent?

The lectionary readings for today are all readings about revenge, or perhaps I should say, revenge and restoration. Micah (4:13) promises that Zion *'shall beat in pieces many peoples …'* and then *'… devote their gain to the Lord'*. Revelation (18:7) looks to the downfall of Babylon as a precursor to the destruction of Rome: *'As she glorified herself and lived luxuriously, so give her a like measure of torment and grief …'* The list of what will happen to the enemy goes on in delightful spite until Revelation 19 when John witnesses rejoicing because God has avenged the blood of God's servants on the enemy (Babylon, Rome, whomever).

I suppose these readings are a not-quite-metaphorical-enough-for-me sug-gestion that the decks need to be cleared in Advent for the coming of

Something New. Decks cleared, punishment levied: Babylon, Rome, populists, conservatives, progressives, foreigners, Trump or Johnson supporters, socialists, evangelicals, police, etc. It is so much easier that way.

It is a nice thought that the bad guys should be washed away. But I am not sure I like that image in the midst of my long-time favourite season of the church year.

For me, there is something fine and hopeful about Advent. I grew up in New England's wonderfully sharp, clear, crisp winter days and bright star-bedecked nights. It is not a time when I think about destruction of anything. Except injustice, I guess. But even with that, Advent has always been more a season of hopeful expectation, not sullied by anger and desire for retribution.

Our late, beloved U.S. Representative John Lewis, friend and colleague of Martin Luther King, Jr., wrote in his 2012 memoir *Across That Bridge: Life Lessons and a Vision for Change*:

> *'Anchor the eternity of love in your own soul and embed this planet with goodness … Release the need to hate, to harbour division, and the enticement of revenge. Release all bitterness. Hold only love, only peace in your heart, knowing that the battle of good to overcome evil is already won.'*[1]

This, from the man who had every excuse to want revenge against the establishment that bloodied his head at the march across the bridge in Selma, Mississippi in 1965, as he was trying to clear the decks of the south from Jim Crow laws. But there was no call in his life, or in the life of Martin Luther King, Jr., to pour out God's anger on the nations.

God clearing the decks for us might seem to make our task to establish justice easier, but I am not convinced that preparation in the days leading up to a celebration of the birth of an embodiment of God's love in the form of a baby should entail making things easier. Instead of obliterating the old, maybe it would be better to use the anticipation of the coming of Something New to strengthen and nurse our hopeful selves, as we wade reflectively into the quagmire of our own past iniquities.

Because it seems to me that we can only call upon God to *'not remember against us the iniquities of our ancestors'* if we have faced and acknowledged those iniquities ourselves. By doing so, our decks are cleared not for retribution, but for God's forgiveness and love.

For many white people, the quagmire of past iniquities must, in 2020, include a good hard look at white privilege. I was brought up by progressive parents in a privileged community. My mother was an activist for civil rights and I remember going to marches in Boston at a very early age. I have continued that legacy, but truthfully, it has only been in the last few months that the Black Lives Matter movement has forced me to more actively read, listen, watch and march myself into a new understanding of how every aspect of my being in the world is assessed and determined by the colour of my skin.

> *'… let your compassion come speedily to meet us, for we are brought very low.'* (Ps 79:8)

Blessedly, there is actually very little talk of revenge these days. Restoration, yes, but not revenge. Restoration of an understanding of human beings as one species. Restoration of a new understanding that the concept of 'race' was largely developed in the 18th century as a sorting of people throughout the colonial empires, a sorting that could then excuse genocide and enslavement.

> *'Hold only love, only peace in your heart, knowing that the battle of good to overcome evil is already won.'* (Rep. John Lewis)

The psalmist, the prophet and the evangelist have it wrong, says John Lewis: *'the battle of good to overcome evil is already won'*.

Restoration without revenge. The birth of Something New.

Prayer:

God alongside us,
take the cancer of revenge and anger in our hearts

and help us to turn it instead
into a growth of a new understanding of our past and present iniquities,
nourished by love and compassion.
Help us to hold only love and peace in our hearts,
our gift, as we journey toward the sacred birth.
Amen

Katharine M Preston

Note:

1. From *Across That Bridge: Life Lessons and a Vision for Change*, John Lewis, Hachette Books, 2012

First Week of Advent, Wednesday

Bible reading:

But you, Bethlehem of Ephratha,
small among Judah's clans,
from you shall come forth for me
one to be ruler in Israel.
His origin lies in former times,
in ancient days.

Micah 5:2[1]

Reflection:

This is probably the most famous verse in Micah, because Matthew quotes it in his birth stories (Mt 2:6) and it is read at every carol service. For Matthew's community, and for generations of Christians, it was a 'proof text' to show that Jesus fulfilled the ancient promises of the prophets. In fact the oracle of which it is part is of completely uncertain date, but deals with the present defeat and humiliation of Judah, and the promise that it will be restored by a leader (*sophet* – the word used for the Judges of Israel) who will not be of David's 'line' – i.e. not descended from David – but will arise as the ancient Judges arose, to lead their people when under threat. *'He shall stand and shepherd in the strength of YHWH, in the majesty of the name of YHWH, his G-d.'* (Mic 5:4)

Matthew's community was not wrong in applying these promises to Reb Joshua ('Jesus') but the radical implications of doing so were often missed. So, as we know, from Constantine onwards (and written into the British coronation service) the royal ideology of the Hebrew Bible was taken over to justify monarchy, hierarchy, and all that goes with it. Handel set the royal psalms to music for the coronation of some of the dimmest and most venal of our monarchs. If, like Paul, however (in Phil 2:5ff), we read the royal psalms, and this promise, through Reb Joshua, then everything goes the other way. Reb Joshua, says Paul, can be addressed by the divine NAME. This redefines everything we think we know about 'rule', leadership and glory – indeed everything we know about G-d. The NAME takes the form of a slave. With that word all the cathedrals, palaces, and the silly nonsense of royal ideology, come crashing to the ground. An end to sycophancy, pomposity, and all the damaging versions of *homo hierarchicus* – whether expressed in caste, class, race or gender. Someone should tell the Church some day …

Because it is Reb Joshua who is the ruler in Israel, the gospel contains a vision of a world made otherwise. From the very first disciples on (Mk 9:32) the promise has seemed impossible, and the church by and large has worshipped the golden calf of the status quo, but Paul got it. In the light of Messiah Jesus, he proclaimed a world where all humans were equal (Gal 3:28); where they lived by solidarity and reciprocity (1 Cor 12); where prayer arose from listening to the groaning of the whole of creation in travail – all the unimaginable pain of evolution and of history, all of the suffering and the needless death, the chaotic blindness of chance (Rom 8); where the cruelty and wickedness of humans was read through the divine solidarity of the cross (Phil 2:8). Because G-d is known in Messiah Jesus, Paul insisted, we can keep the vision alive, can keep on hoping despite the mendacity and wickedness of rulers, and despite our own folly and blindness, can keep praying for G-d's kingly rule as Reb Joshua wanted us to, can keep trying to live as if the world really was turned upside down. Those who did that, and sought to live by that vision, he called – probably following Reb Joshua himself (Mt 16:18) – 'ekklesia'.

Prayer:

Spirit of God,
rescue us from despair,
give us hope,
help us to live according to your promise
of a world made otherwise.

Tim Gorringe

Note:

1. Translation of Micah, by James Luther Mays, SCM, 1976

First Week of Advent, Thursday

Bible reading:

Steadfast love and faithfulness will meet;
  righteousness and peace will kiss each other.
Faithfulness will spring up from the ground,
  and righteousness will look down from the sky.

Psalm 85:10–11 (NRSV)

Reflection:

The opening responses in the Iona Abbey morning service are inspired by this psalm:

The world belongs to God,
the earth and all its people.

How good it is, how wonderful,
to live together in unity.

Love and faith come together,
justice and peace join hands.[1]

Meeting, embracing, kissing, holding hands … How strange the physicality of this feels just now, in days when the discipline of distancing has become part of our daily lives. For most of 2020, the instinct to hug has been held in check. While there are many ways to express belonging together, some are tactile, and just now these can be a no-go area. But our bodies remember.

Only a few months ago, things were so different. What has happened? We remember when we took for granted spending time and literally being in touch with people we love, with whom we share a worldview: love and faith naturally coming together. It can hurt to remember that now.

One day this summer I talked on the phone with two friends, older than me and much wiser. They are both people for whom I feel love and respect. Their homes are miles apart. I talked with them separately. Each has lived – in different ways – a commitment to justice for those that our society treats as outsiders: through hospitality and practical support, through raising the theological questions we all need to face. Among the things the three of us have in common is the memory of joining in with those responses in Abbey worship many, many times:

How good it is, how wonderful,
to live together in unity.

The telephone is a gift at a time when meeting face to face or mingling our voices isn't possible. On the day of the calls, each friend had different things to share. One is recently bereaved, reflecting in that rawness what the loss of someone so precious means in a world that still *'belongs to God'*. One is struggling with anxiety, deepened by isolation, about a different loss – of short-term memory.

The first told me about words which had helped him, and they came to mind in the conversation with that other mutual friend. The quotation came from Dietrich Bonhoeffer's *Letters and Papers from Prison*:

'Gratitude changes the pangs of memory to a tranquil joy.'

When I put the phone down, I reflected:

Pangs of memory
are like a wound that won't heal;
sometimes, too, there's that dull ache
of something just not there any more.

Right now, this is too real –
when so much else has changed,
while we go on living between the gaps
where names and words should be.

Doubting ourselves,
we know it's dishonest to conceal
the pain of loss and fear of what comes next:
another day, another empty day.

Remembering how we once took on the world –
joyfully, hand in hand – wondering now
how do we face these storms alone?

How can we cope with such extremes of weather –
tempest and flood and drought –
raging within as well as out –
confused and grieving through the night,
our spirits at their lowest point, always alone.

Yet gratitude has the power to transform,
like spring sunshine touching the cold earth.
A memory like dawn breaking,
for those who rise, step into the first rays of light,
see dew glittering on the grass, feel
the young sun's warmth, the air's caress,
smell moist and fertile earth, taste salt air,
and, with familiar words, hear echoes of a loved voice,
remember a smile.

Shared commitment, ground of common faith,
salted with blessing: the gift of gratitude,
for lives that touched us, shaped us, who knows how,
with whom God's love unites us, here and now.

Prayer:

Thank you, God, for the things that give life meaning,
for memories healed and words that unite.
Thank you for the transforming power
of justice and peace, faith and love –

not as abstractions, but joyfully down-to-earth,
met in people who are made in your image
and embody your love, hands-on.
Thank you for shared commitment to justice,
and companionship in seeking peace. **Amen**

Jan Sutch Pickard

Note:

1. From *Iona Abbey Worship Book*, Wild Goose Publications, 2017

First Week of Advent, Friday

Bible reading:

... among them were some men of Cyprus and Cyrene who, on coming to Antioch, spoke to the Hellenists also, proclaiming the Lord Jesus ... it was in Antioch that the disciples were first called 'Christians'.

Acts 11:20,26 (NRSV)

Reflection:

Divisions, barriers, borders: there were plenty of them in the ancient world; and there are plenty of them now. When the Book of Acts registers the appearance of a brand-new word, 'Christians', to describe the new disciples in Antioch, it seems almost a throwaway remark. But it marks a *kairos* moment, decisive and challenging, a moment when everything began to change.

In the first century (and long before it), the Greeks had always seen themselves as superior to other peoples – the 'barbarians'. And citizens of the Roman Empire had political and legal rights that were denied to slaves or women or the poor. Famously St Paul makes the most of his rights as a Roman citizen. And then there were Aramaic-speaking Jews in Judaea and Palestine, and Greek-speaking Jews living dispersed in the towns and cities around the Mediterranean, but especially in Alexandria in Egypt and in Antioch in what is now Turkey, very close to the Syrian border. And of course there were the *goyim* – the other nations who weren't Jewish that we so easily lump together as the Gentiles. Jews and Gentiles, Greeks and barbarians, Roman citizens and the subjects of the Empire without the same rights. In such a divided world, the movement started by Jesus began to spread.

It began with persecution that sent believers through the eastern Mediterranean (Phoenicia, Cyprus) right into Antioch, the Roman capital of the province of 'Syria'. And that's where a new thing happened. That's where the breakthrough came. Instead of just sharing their story of resurrection and new life with the local Jewish congregations, some of the disciples from Cyprus and Cyrene broke ranks, broke the rule, crossed the line and spoke to *'the Hellenists'* – Greek speakers who were not Jewish. As a result, the faith spread rapidly in Antioch; the leadership in Jerusalem sent in Barnabas to see what was going on, and he in turn enlisted St Paul. But it's not just a new brand – 'Christians' – that is created. It's a new freedom.

In a time when the Empire used citizenship rules to decide who was in and who was out, Jesus' people don't just cross political or geographical borders, they break through the barriers of old thinking. Their energy, their enthusiasm, *'proclaiming the Lord Jesus'*, carries them beyond the carefully observed limits and all the traditional categories that guaranteed the status quo, that secured Roman political power just as much as they bolstered religious authorities and their control. The message of Jesus took them beyond the old mindset and into a new world. They just couldn't stop themselves.

And how about our barriers, and borders, and boundaries? Separation walls in Israel/Palestine, the USA's border wall, the UK Border Force? We have plenty of labels too: economic migrant, illegal immigrant, asylum seeker, refugee. Even the very things that make us who we are – gay/straight, black/white, cis and trans – get turned into hostile borders. Will *'proclaiming the Lord Jesus'* like those who were first called 'Christians' challenge us to break the barriers and open the borders? They are barriers and blockages in minds and hearts, every bit as much as citizenship rules that ignore human need and leave children to drown.

May God give us the fire and energy that carried Christians beyond all the divisions of the past to the beginnings of a new world.

In her poem 'Cross-border peace talks', Kathy Galloway writes:

There is a place
beyond the borders
where love grows …

It is not an easy place to be,
this place beyond the borders.
It is where you learn that there is more pain in love than in hate,
more courage in forbearance than in vengeance,
more remembering needed in forgetting,
and always new borders to cross.

But it is a good place to be.[1]

Tony Phelan

Note:

1. Kathy Galloway, from *The Dream of Learning Our True Name*, Kathy Galloway, Wild Goose Publications, 2004

First Week of Advent, Saturday

Bible reading:

'I will take you from the nations, and gather you from all the countries, and bring you into your own land. I will sprinkle clean water upon you, and you shall be clean from all your uncleannesses, and from all your idols I will cleanse you. A new heart I will give you, and a new spirit I will put within you; and I will remove from your body the heart of stone and give you a heart of flesh.'

Ezekiel 36:24–26 (NRSV)

Reflection:

As a pastor, I have lost count over the years of the number of times someone has said to me something along the lines of, *'I am a person of faith, but I just cannot stand the Old Testament. It is filled with so much violence, destruction, death and cruelty. And don't get me started on the God of the Old Testament!'*

I have to say I understand those sentiments – there is much in the Old Testament to turn off believers. We can say it's because of the time in which it was written, but that can be a weak excuse.

Yet, as I grow older, I am drawn more and more to the Old Book. If we pay close attention, and get past all those exaggerated claims of victories against staggering odds, we *do* discover a God of grace, of hope, of love, of peace. In the midst of all the dire warnings in the prophets, we discover those marvellous gems in Hosea, Isaiah, Jeremiah and Habakkuk, which tell us of a compassionate and caring God.

The reading from Ezekiel here is another marvellous example. It is written to a people who are in exile and perched on the very edge of despair. Their spirits have turned to ashes, their dreams are gone, and their hearts have turned to stone. They are bitter, alone, forgotten. And what does God say through the prophet?

'I am coming for you, to bring you back home.'

No words of judgement. No reminder that they have brought this down upon themselves. No 'clean up your act, and then I might notice you again'. No.

God plans to act in a completely unexpected way. God is coming to save the people. Why? Because that is what God does. That is what God's holiness is all about. Not anger, vengeance, punishment – but justice, hope, healing, restoration. That God is present from the very beginning of scripture to the very end.

And if you think that these verses are not important to our faith, well, just remember that Jesus grew up with these verses and other words from the Old Testament about God coming to save, about God putting new spirits into our empty souls, about God cracking open our hearts of stone so those of joy might emerge. And maybe from verses like this, Jesus learned of a God of grace, of hope, of love, of justice, of peace. The God he showed to us through his birth, which we await; his life, which we will follow once again in the coming months; his spirit which makes our spirits new; his heart which mends our broken hearts.

Prayer:

In this year of uncertainty,
in this time of so much
anger, hate and fear,
we could respond with
coldness and indifference
to the gifts of grace
you offer to us,

so give us that new heart
promised so long ago,
fill us with that new spirit
which we need more
than ever before.

Thom M Shuman

Second Sunday of Advent

Bible reading: Mark 1:1–18

Reflection:

Scene 1. Brook St, Mayfair, Central London. 1741.

A man paces around his London home, worried about his future, struggling with his health. A successful composer, he is not good at business and recently avoided debtors' prison. He's thinking of giving up. He paces his room and thinks: 'Maybe something will turn up.' He can only wait.

Scene 2: Jordan River, Palestine. 27 AD. (Roughly).

Another hot and dusty day and the eccentric preacher, who shouts at everyone, has drawn a crowd.

'Prepare the way,' he tells them. 'Get your act together. It's about to happen. Any day now.'

Anna stops beating her washing on the sun-baked rocks, and turns to Ruth. 'Wouldn't it be great if it was true?'

'If what was true?'

'If it was true that all this waiting was over, that soon we will know the glory of God ...'

The women look up from their washing at the sound of laughing and cheering as the preacher-man pushes someone else under the water and hauls them up. 'Prepare the way of the Lord!' he shouts.

Scene 3. Three and a half thousand years before Scene 2. (Roughly).

In the Bronze Age someone has learned how to write: Sumerian cuneiform script, Egyptian hieroglyphics. Later, in the town of Nippur, in the country we now call Iraq, now only a millennia and a half before Scene 2, someone will scratch symbols on a tablet. The notation indicates names of strings on a lyre. This tablet is the earliest representation of a recorded melody ever found. Someone has learned how to take the melody they hear in their head, the one they hum as they walk or prepare food, and visualise it. Someone has learned how to write out music and share it with someone else.

Scene 4. Brook St, Mayfair, London. 1741.

For the worried man the waiting is about to end. A friend gives him some words, like a poem, written for performance, often called a libretto. Words from the Bible. A preacher telling anyone who will listen that their waiting is over.

'Prepare the way of the Lord, make his paths straight.'

The preacher quotes another preacher, who was waiting 700 years before. *'And the glory of the Lord shall be revealed, and all flesh shall see it …'*

Something clicks in the mind of the worried man. He begins to hear it. Something no one else has ever heard. What it might sound like when the way is prepared and God finally arrives.

Thanks to the Sumerians and Egyptians, thanks to the ancient Iraqi in Nippur, thanks to Isaiah the Prophet and the Baptist John. Thanks to people who had been waiting long before he was waiting, the worried man begins to write down what he hears. Within 24 days he has committed everything he can hear to 260 pages of manuscript.

Tears streaming down his face, George Frederick Handel gives his new work a title. He calls it *Messiah*.

Scene 5. Anywhere. Anytime.

We are all waiting.

Some people are waiting to find out if they've got a job. Or the money for their rent. Some people are waiting for good news on a loved one.

Some people are waiting for someone to listen to them. Some people are waiting for inspiration. Some people are waiting to find that special person. Some people are waiting to be asked.

We are all always waiting for something else. For someone to prepare the way. To see the glory of God. For freedom to ring.

For justice to roll down like a river.

For the world to stop warming. For a vaccine. For the exiled to gain entry, for the powerful to lay power down.

Sometimes what we are waiting for has already arrived.

In 1741 George Frederick Handel doesn't know he is waiting for the arrival of writing, the evolution of instruments, the invention of composition. He takes for granted all the waiting of everyone who has gone before him. The prophet in the 7th century BC doesn't know he is waiting for Jesus Christ. We do not know who is preparing the way or who will show up when it is ready.

We do not know what will come at the end of our waiting. None of us know how all of us will see the glory of the Lord. But the glory is always there, waiting to be revealed.

What is it we are waiting for when we say we are waiting for the way to be prepared? When we are waiting to see the glory, the glory, the glory of the Lord? Sometimes, the answer is that we are waiting for ourselves.

Sometimes while we are waiting for God … God is waiting for us.

Martin Wroe

Second Week of Advent, Monday

Bible reading:

> *The Lord is my light and my salvation;*
> *whom shall I fear?*
> *The Lord is the stronghold of my life;*
> *of whom shall I be afraid? …*

> *Teach me your way, O Lord,*
> *and lead me on a level path*
> *because of my enemies.*
> *Do not give me up to the will of my adversaries,*
> *for false witnesses have risen against me,*
> *and they are breathing out violence.*

> *I believe that I shall see the goodness of the Lord*
> *in the land of the living.*
> *Wait for the Lord;*
> *be strong, and let your heart take courage;*
> *wait for the Lord!*

Psalm 27:1,11–14 (NRSV)

Reflection:

The psalmist believes she will see the goodness of the Lord while she is alive. The psalmist has not seen goodness yet, but believes that she will if she waits long enough.

But the world we live in can soon lose its joy, with war and violence, hate and injustice. For some time now, an unrelenting virus has haunted us with sickness and death. And there are other viruses that take their toll on our lives. Reckless people who promote conflict and chaos disrupt our lives, hurting us and all creation. In the land where I live, the millstone of racism has weighed heavy on necks for centuries.

Yet, my heart is not discouraged. Voices rise from every land, teaching us the way of the Lord. Together we can redeem the places where we live and the relationships we build, if we would be strong, fill our hearts with courage, and wait for the Lord! Of course, waiting is an ambiguous action. Some say do nothing, leave things the way they are, because God will take care of everything. But only the fear-filled observer does nothing when the house is on fire.

The psalmist's words rain down, *'The Lord is my light and my salvation; whom shall I fear?'* Think of all the confusing messages we get in the course of a day. What if we followed our fear and never listened to God or the voice of reason? As Christians, we have a moral obligation to do something when goodness is suppressed. If we are to right the wrongs of history, we cannot wait and do nothing. Waiting in prayer and acting in love go hand in hand. With God as our light and the stronghold of our lives, we can make the land of the living a beloved community, a world at peace on earth as in heaven.

There is goodness in the land of the living – there always has been. Simeon knew he had seen the goodness of the Lord in the temple when he held Jesus in his arms (Lk 2:30). Elizabeth, too, knew she was in the presence of goodness, even before Jesus was born (Lk 1:41).

Simeon and Elizabeth were ordinary people who had extraordinary vision. In their waiting, they had the courage to recognise the gift of salvation, and they opened their hearts to receive its light.

There are ordinary people with extraordinary vision among us, who remind us the light of God is with us even in our fear. After a lifetime of working for justice, the U.S. congressman John Lewis encouraged Americans, from his deathbed: *'together, you can redeem the soul of our nation,'*[1] through non-violent action, in spite of fear.

During a CT scan for a health scare, a dear friend, scholar and modern-day mystic told me she prayed for the presence of beloved people to come near and sustain her. One who came was Julian of Norwich, saying *'all will be well,'* and offered her a vision of being intimately connected with God, as though she was floating in God's womb.

When a young climate activist from Sweden faced her adversaries on the urgency of acting to stop global warming, I was inspired with hope once again. Greta Thunberg, a teenager, could not keep silent when she saw our world house on fire. She was strong and her heart took courage when she accused world leaders of ignoring the science behind the global climate crisis.

And, again, *'a little child shall lead them'* (Is 11:6), as teenagers did in Parkland, Florida, when they protested for gun control in a nation where guns are 'sacrosanct'.

These people's prayers and actions, in the face of fear, inspire me and give me hope. Their visions of a better future give me courage to wait in the strength of prayer and to act in love.

So, in this holy season before the arrival of Christ in our midst, my heart is not discouraged – for hope is being born in us and among us, over and over again. With the Lord as our light and salvation, whom shall we fear? We remind each other that God is with us in the land of the living. We show each other that God is our stronghold, even in our fear, whatever and wherever it may be: Covid time, virtual space …

We all have the opportunity to wait and work for a beloved world community by sowing seeds of goodness. We begin by renewing ourselves (and all creation) in the image of God by the way we live. How do you, an ordinary person, do that? As goodness in the land of the living shows us, you begin today, right here, right now, right where you are, in prayer and protest, contemplation and action. Whatever path we choose to wait for the Lord, it is our spiritual path, and will lead us to a better way, the way of goodness.

Praying in love with love

So much sadness, so much sorrow
praying for tomorrow.

We help each other
loving what God loves.

We hurt each other
breathing out violence.

Time passes anyway
and goodness happens every day.

Hope restores the soul
while storms take their toll.

Waking to each morning,
there is fear and warning.

Sounds are made
and silence stayed.

Yet truer than all truth we know
love will grow and continue on to flow.

Rebeka Maples

Note:

1. From 'Together, you can redeem the soul of our nation,' John Lewis, *New York Times*, 30 July, 2020

Second Week of Advent, Tuesday

Bible reading:

As I looked at it closely I saw four-footed animals, birds of prey, reptiles, and birds of the air. I also heard a voice saying to me, 'Get up, Peter; kill and eat.' But I replied, 'By no means, Lord; for nothing unclean or profane has ever entered my mouth.' But a second time the voice answered from heaven, 'What God has called clean, you must not call profane.'

Acts 11:6–9 (NRSV)

Reflection:

'For many of you Stella was a Christian. For us she was a Sikh. Like water, she took the shape of the bottle she was in.' The words of the Scottish Sikh leader Mr Balwant Singh Saggu, at the funeral of Stella Reekie, Deaconess of the Church of Scotland, in October 1982.

When Stella returned from her time as a missionary in Pakistan, she developed a unique ministry of companionship, particularly in her home in Glasgow, which became known as the International Flat. There groups of women, often newly arrived from Asia, and so many others, women and men of diverse backgrounds, experienced enrichment in their lives. The 'Sharing of Faiths' programme expressed Stella's conviction that true dialogue required openness to learn and be changed. It was not always popular within her own Church of Scotland, where some considered that Mr Saggu's tribute indicated that she had diluted her own faith.

Nothing could be further from the truth for this evangelical Christian who was so open to discovering God in all people, simply because of the depth of her allegiance to Jesus.

The gospel writers cite Peter amongst the first and closest followers of Jesus, with all too many human flaws. In Antioch, in a dispute with Paul, he refused to associate with Gentiles who were ritually 'unclean', unless they became Jews through circumcision. In the strange dream that he had in

Joppa, he was horrified at the idea of eating creatures forbidden in the law of Moses. G.W.H. Lampe, a New Testament scholar, linked this learning vision to the issue of 'table fellowship'. Eating together in the Middle East was such a sacred act, he wrote, that rather than focusing on eating banned birds or reptiles, this passage was really about giving or receiving hospitality with the 'profane', and now in the Christian era, sharing the Lord's Supper with them.[1]

The doctrine of Apartheid originated, not in the political victory of the Nationalist Party in 1948 in South Africa, but in the Dutch Reformed Church towards the end of the 19th century. Congregations in the Cape were permitted to hold separate communion services for Africans and Europeans on the spurious grounds of the 'tender consciences' of white members who refused to sit at the Lord's Table with those of a race that, for them, God had created to be inferior. That doctrine, which gave spiritual support to a system of racial oppression, was finally declared a basic heresy over a century later by the World Alliance of Reformed Churches, and a fundamental barrier to fellowship in the wider Christian communion for any church which practised it.

Jesus once spoke about a small mustard seed growing to become a bush in which the birds nested. The plant was seen as a weed in Palestine, and it was uprooted to preserve more 'useful' ones. It has been suggested that some of the very birds that found shelter there were those termed unclean in religious law. Could it be that the great storyteller deliberately used a despised plant that sheltered 'unclean' creatures, to teach his listeners about the surprising inclusivity of God?

George More, a late member of the Iona Community, who, like Stella Reekie, served the Church in Asia for many years, used to confess that when he first went to India shortly after the Second World War, he fondly cherished the illusion that he was 'bringing God to India'. 'Gradually,' he said, 'I developed the strong conviction that God was saying to me "George, I have been here for thousands of years. Your job is to discover what I am doing in the lives of the people."' For thirty years George More became immersed in rural India with an unconditional ministry, discovering what God was doing, beyond credal and other barriers.

Prayer:

God of contrasts,
of light and shade, of the kaleidoscope of cultures and faiths,
present in the wildness of the wind
and the calm after the storm,
you are present in our own stormy moments
and in the stillness of our quiet times.

When the sun wakes us from our nightmares or our sweet dreams,
you are there, welcoming us with the gift of a new day,
challenging us with its promise and possibilities.

When times are hard, and we would rather go back to sleep,
hold us fast, in your light and shade,
show us that we are never alone.
Remind us that others in their different struggles need our support.
And as you travel the road with us –
let us travel the road with others: strangers and friends;
listening to their stories, understanding their needs,
and then we will know that as we meet you in our companions,
so also will we be met.

When we have avoided the rocky road of another's struggles,
when we have turned and looked away,
forgive us and show us that your way is our way;
let us all travel together in light and shade,
in stormy and in calm weather,
in shared understanding and in shared humanity,
always remembering the open companionship that Jesus shared.

Iain and Isabel Whyte

Note:

1. G.W.H. Lampe, in a section on Luke's Gospel in *Peake's Commentary on the Bible*, Thomas Nelson, 1967

Second Week of Advent, Wednesday

Bible reading:

Hear, O Lord, when I cry aloud,
*   be gracious to me and answer me!*
'Come,' my heart says, 'seek his face!'
*   Your face, Lord, do I seek.*
*   Do not hide your face from me.*

Do not turn your servant away in anger,
*   you who have been my help.*
Do not cast me off, do not forsake me,
*   O God of my salvation!*
If my father and mother forsake me,
*   the Lord will take me up.*

Teach me your way, O Lord,
*   and lead me on a level path*
*   because of my enemies.*

Psalm 27:7–11 (NRSV)

Reflection:

This account is true, though the names have been changed. 'Chidubem' means 'Guided by God'.

'Hi, I'm from the Chaplaincy. I've been asked to come and see Danny Chidubem.'

'Er, yeh, Chidubem; he's in C12, I'll take you up,' replied the prison officer.

The young offenders institution, at which I volunteer, is home to 650 young men aged between 18 and 25.

Of course, all victims of crime must be our priority. Physical injury or psychological trauma damages lives. Having spoken to many individuals, I know, only too well, how devastating it is to be a victim of crime. All victims need our practical support and must be included in our daily prayers. But, in my view, there are also forgotten victims ... victims of society.

To place teens and young men behind a 20-foot brick wall and ignore them has never sat comfortably with me. Yes, I know all the arguments. Protection of the public and the need for rehabilitation, but the words of Jesus have rung in my ears for decades:

'And when I was in prison, you visited me.' (Mt 25:36).

I arrived at cell C12.

'I'll leave you with him then,' said the officer.

'OK, thanks. Hi, Danny, my name is Peter. I'm from the Chaplaincy.'

Before me sat a 19-year-old black youth. He was gazing at the floor.

He was just a few years younger than my own son, but in very different circumstances.

'How's it going then, Danny?'

'OK,' came the reply, but there was no eye contact.

'So where do you come from, Danny?'

' ... Lewisham.'

'Lewisham ... Hmm, I got a parking ticket there once.'

Danny looked up. 'Do you know Lewisham then?'

'A bit.'

'St Mark's Road ... do you know it?'

I owned up and said I didn't, but at least a thin wafer of conversation had begun. It turned out Danny's parents had split up when he was four. He had been brought up by his mother, until she could no longer cope. He went into care when he was 10 and had to be housed in North London.

Expelled from school at the age of 15, he had drifted into a particularly brutal London gang.

Over the next few months, I made a point of seeing Danny at least once a week. On week three, he smiled at me. On week five, he asked me another question!

'What happens in the chapel then?'

'Well,' I said, 'each Sunday we have a church service, which is led by different folk. Then, in the week, we have Bible study groups and music groups, and we even have a quiz morning … Would you be interested?'

Danny explained that he used to go to chapel with his grandmother, but hadn't been near a chapel or church since he was six years old.

Back at the Chaplaincy Office that day, the Managing Chaplain said, 'It's your turn to preach in two weeks' time, Peter. Is that OK?'

'OK.'

The day came for me to preach in front of 60 prisoners. To my surprise and delight, Danny was amongst them. He gave me the thumbs up as I went up to the desk.

I began to talk about Psalm 27, and about the Crucifixion: about how, on the cross, the arms of Jesus were outstretched … and still today, his arms are outstretched, to receive each one of us. No matter who we are, Jesus opens his arms for us.

In Psalm 27:7 we ask the Lord to *'Hear my voice'*; and in verse 9, *'Do not leave me or forsake me, God of my salvation.'* In verse 10: *'Though my father and mother forsake me, the Lord will take me up.'*

I glanced at Danny in the third row. His eyes were welling up. The guy next to him put an arm around him in comfort.

I concluded my sermon by saying: 'No matter who we are, no matter what our life has been, Jesus loves us and *will* be our guide for ever.'

Prayer:

Lord Jesus, in the agony of the day,
you opened wide your arms upon the cross.
In humility, we come to you today,
and ask you to embrace us in your loving arms.

Comfort all victims of crime,
that they may recover from trauma.
Sustain those who work for our protection.
Walk with those who have taken the wrong path
and bring them back into the fold.
Forgive us all for our inadequacies.
And, Lord Jesus, help us to reform our communities
so we may all live in peace and security.

These things we ask in your Holy Name.
Amen

Peter Phillips

Second Week of Advent, Thursday

Bible reading:

I want to know Christ and the power of his resurrection and the sharing of his sufferings by becoming like him in his death, if somehow I may attain the resurrection from the dead.

Philippians 3:10–11 (NRSV)

Reflection:

Paul wrote his letter to the Philippians while he was in prison on account of his faith. He seeks to encourage the members of the church at Philippi in their faith because they are also facing opposition. Paul assures the Philippians that his imprisonment is not hindering his mission – and he tells them that the gospel is spreading even among the imperial guard.

Today's reading comes from the central section of the letter in which Paul speaks of the power of *'knowing Christ'*. In some ways it is a strange passage for Advent but Paul's imprisonment leads him to reflect on his faith, and in Advent we are also reflecting on our faith and the impact of Christ coming into the world.

Paul speaks of the way in which his faith in Christ has led to a reorientation of his life. In the verses before our reading Paul describes his heritage. He is a member of the people of Israel and the tribe of Benjamin; he was a Pharisee and considered righteous according to the Law but he persecuted the church. He now believes that his former status, authority and power have no value; that everything in his life may be regarded as *'loss'* when seen in the light of the *'surpassing value of knowing Christ'*.

Paul's very personal letter demonstrates his close relationship with the members of the church in Philippi. The Philippians heard that Paul is in prison, and sent one of their members, Epaphroditus, to bring gifts to Paul. Epaphroditus has been ill during his visit and almost died. The Philippians have been worried about him, and he is now returning to Philippi with Paul's letter.

Although Paul is in prison and the Philippians are suffering persecution, Philippians is a joyful letter which expresses Paul's confidence in Christ. Paul urges the Philippians to *'rejoice in the Lord always'*, and tells them that *'the Lord is near'*. They are experiencing opposition on earth, but their *'citizenship is in heaven'*, he says. Paul wants the Philippians to be confident that the world will be brought under the authority of Christ.

Paul does not know whether he will live or die but tells the Philippians that what is important is knowing Christ. He asks the Philippians to have the *'same mind'* as Christ. In Philippians 2, he cites an early Christian hymn which describes the Incarnation. The hymn states that Christ was in the form of God but emptied himself and took the form of a servant. Then Christ experienced death and was exalted by God.

Paul seeks to imitate Christ by sharing in his sufferings, in the hope that he might also share in the power of the Resurrection.

Paul lives in a time of fear and uncertainty but he waits for Christ.

In Advent, we are also waiting for Christ to come into places of fear and uncertainty: into our own fearful and uncertain lives; and into places like detention centres and prisons.

Think about those around the world who are imprisoned because of their faith or political beliefs.

Think about refugees, some of them children, detained in detention centres.

Prayer:

Gracious Christ,
you come among us,
born as one of us.

You come among us
bringing new life into dark places.

With the power of the Resurrection
you transform us and change the world.

Action: www.amnesty.org.uk

Susan Miller

Second Week of Advent, Friday

Bible reading:

When the Lord restored the fortunes of Zion,
  we were like those who dream.
Then our mouth was filled with laughter,
  and our tongue with shouts of joy;
then it was said among the nations,
'The Lord has done great things for them.'

Psalm 126:1–2 (NRSV)

Reflection:

Even if we are not familiar with many of the Psalms, this one may be known to us. It has been put to music many times through the generations. For centuries it has been one of the Psalms at the core of the Advent readings in the world church. It is not difficult to understand why it is placed firmly within the pre-Christmas Bible readings. One of the central themes in this particular psalm is that of 'looking forward' of 'expectancy'. I understand that to mean that the pilgrims collectively were holding in their hearts and minds a profound hope concerning the guidance of God within their many human journeys. And in traditional church teaching this psalm is also understood to be looking forward to the coming of a Saviour into the world – although that actual coming took place a long time after this psalm was written, possibly by Ezra hundreds of years before the birth of Jesus. What we do know with some degree of certainty is that this psalm is number seven in the great series of fifteen pilgrim songs, used by the pilgrims on their way to Jerusalem: sung in joy on their ascent to Zion. Thus taken together as a group, they are always referred to as the Songs of Ascent.

Some people, when reading a passage from scripture, find it quite easy to imagine themselves within, say, a first-century situation in a Palestinian village. They can know at an emotional and spiritual level what it was to be one of the crowd as Jesus passed by on the road. I have never been able to have that kind of imaginative understanding of a Bible story but I do connect with the hopes and dreams of the pilgrims as they made their song-filled walk to Jerusalem. They were walking together with souls full of gratitude for the way in which their God had led them out of exile into a new future in their own land.

This return from exile, at the time of Ezra and Nehemiah, was a truly liberating experience. It was the kind of transformative experience for which millions in our world today long for every day of their lives. That movement from captivity of one kind or another, into a place where a human being can feel the fresh air of freedom, is a journey the oppressed and abandoned in 2020 dream about. It is not surprising that these pilgrims centuries ago had much to sing about. They knew that the Lord had done great things for them and they knew how to celebrate that fact. In this beautiful psalm we also read these uplifting words: '*May those who sow in tears reap with shouts of joy. Those who go out weeping, bearing the seed for sowing, shall come home with shouts of joy carrying their sheaves.*' (Ps 126:5–6, NRSV)

It is exactly this sense of God-infused longing and expectancy that we are invited to hold in our spiritual depths as we come again to rejoice in the birth of Jesus. In our turbulent, fearful world, much of which is now under the rule of dictators, may we have the courage to witness through our lives to that great truth that '*this* is *the day the Lord gives us and we can rejoice in it*'.

Prayer:

Lord, let me walk today with all the dreamers
who still believe
that God's goodness and justice,
forgiveness and love
are present on earth.

Peter Millar

Second Week of Advent, Saturday

Bible reading:

… 'A man had two sons; he went to the first and said, "Son, go and work in the vineyard today." He answered, "I will not"; but later he changed his mind and went. The father went to the second and said the same; and he answered, "I go, sir"; but he did not go. Which of the two did the will of his father?' They said, 'The first.' Jesus said to them, 'Truly I tell you, the tax collectors and the prostitutes are going into the kingdom of God ahead of you. For John came to you in the way of righteousness and you did not believe him, but the tax collectors and the prostitutes believed him; and even after you saw it, you did not change your minds and believe him …'

Matthew 21:28–32 (NRSV)

Reflection:

On a hill in the city of Edinburgh proudly stands a beautiful, historic church – the Greyfriars Kirk. Just down the hill from it is its humbler sister, as it might seem: the Grassmarket Community Project.[1] Humble it might be, but it holds a golden heart.

I talked to a friend recently and he was complaining about his 'wayward' son. He said he wondered about taking him somewhere like the Grassmarket Project, to 'show him where things could end up'. That stopped me in my tracks. To see the Project as a deterrent example!

In fact, it is exactly as in the Bible reading – the people we do not expect to be the ones to 'enter the kingdom of God' actually do the right thing, do what the 'Father wants', are where God is present and acting – and are the very foretaste of the kingdom.

Yes, many people who come to the Project have addiction issues. Some have had a brush with the law sometime in their lives. Others live with long-term illness or are recovering after a stroke. Many are foreigners in the country. Many struggle with mental health. Many are poor and live on benefits. But the Grassmarket Project is one of the most wonderful places I have ever experienced.

People care for and about each other and the environment. Nobody is judged for what they cannot do. Everybody is welcomed and supported. People find belonging after long isolation. People learn new skills that they can use in work life, or just for fun. There is a gardening group, a choir, an art group, a wood workshop, writing, mindfulness, positive mental health, cooking and other classes. People come together to eat, to celebrate and to become a community.

Last Christmas we prepared a Christmas play by telling each other stories: stories about kindness, about being taken into people's homes in winter-time after losing a room in a hostel. Stories of sharing and of humanity.

This year we planted a fruit orchard in the kirkyard, including the Peace Tree planted together with the Sikh community.

Recently a group of six from the Grassmarket Project went to Zambia to help build a school for girls in a remote, rural area. They did sleep-outs and other fundraising and gathered the money for the trip themselves. Some had never been outside Scotland; some had never been outside Edinburgh. Some struggled with addictions, some with mental health issues. But they did it! And it changed their lives. They had thought they were poor and disadvantaged. Now they saw that having running water is a privilege. They saw that they had so much – enough to live well. But, best of all, they saw that they can do something and be welcomed and cherished by people. The children especially loved them!

Prayer:

Jesus Christ, servant of the poor,
friend of the outcast,
hope for the criminal and the condemned,
healer of the broken,
family to the unwanted,
you were a refugee in Egypt,
you had no place to lay your head,
you thirsted while tortured on the cross.

Open our hearts and minds
to embrace the unwanted,
to honour the lowly,
to welcome the outcast,
to see the value and dignity of all,
to become a community with each other,
to build a just society with wellbeing and a place for all.
Amen

Urzula Glienecke

Note:

1. The Grassmarket Community Project has been developed in partnership by Greyfriars Kirk (Church of Scotland) and the Grassmarket Mission ... The Project offers a mixture of education programmes, drop-in services, social enterprise and social integration activities. Though founded on work with those traditionally labelled 'homeless', this project has been extended to adults who have been marginalised by lack of opportunity, skills and aspiration (from the Grassmarket Community Project website: *http://grassmarket.org*).

Third Sunday of Advent

He has brought down the powerful from their thrones,
      and lifted up the lowly;
he has filled the hungry with good things,
      and sent the rich away empty.

Luke 1:52–53 (NRSV)

Reflection:

It feels pretty wrong to write about Mary's song, as a man. OK, well, as a trans man. OK, so maybe it's not wrong at all, because I have lived as a woman, I had a womb … Too much information? That's the thing. People who have suffered oppression are often on the defensive, feeling the need to justify ourselves before we even start to speak.

So what about Mary? We know that she was a young, unmarried woman. People have made much of her age, but we mustn't get too stuck in our own culture. For Mary, getting married at the age of 13 or so would have been perfectly normal. The thing is, she wasn't married yet and she was already pregnant. That puts Mary right at the centre of a very big, very frightening target.

Fast forward a few decades and Jesus meets another young woman in a very similar situation. She is surrounded by a circle of angry, jeering men holding the heavy stones that they intend to throw at her; she is accused of adultery; it's likely that she's pregnant, unless a man has been caught in the act of raping her, and she is getting the blame. Jesus kneels down and writes in the sand. I wonder if that act of gentle mercy is, in part, inspired by a vision of his mother 30 years before.

Mary, narrowly escaping the accusatory blows of stoning, expresses the Magnificat to her kin, Elizabeth. She speaks truth to power from a place of oppression and, surely, fear. We often read this song as an expression of joy; but could it actually be the song of the oppressed and afraid? Could it be a song of justification and hope? Could it be that Mary is humbly suggesting that people who have been oppressed and cast out to the margins can carry God's Good News of liberation, freedom and rebirth for all?

Surely, as a young, unmarried, brown, immigrant woman riding miles and miles on a donkey whilst heavily pregnant, Mary has something in common with those who are persecuted, oppressed and marginalised today.

In Mary's youth, she shares experiences with all those whose wisdom is ignored because they are supposedly 'too young', or 'too old'. In Mary's unmarried pregnancy, she shares experiences with all those who have been shunned, cast out or abused because of their gender or sexuality. In Mary's long and dangerous journey, she shares experiences with all those who have had to seek refuge in another land. In Mary's physical discomfort on her journey, she shares experiences with all those whose bodies ache and groan. In Mary's brown skin, she embodies the message that Black Lives Matter.

As a transmasculine person, I feel immense hope every time I read or hear Mary's song. It often feels as though those who have power have a lot of control over my life and the lives of trans people around the world. Like Mary, trans people have experienced censure and opposition from religious, cultural and political forces. Many religious bodies teach that it is sinful to be trans. Stoning of trans people is still practised in several countries, as would have been the punishment had Mary been found guilty of adultery. We still face abuse in the streets and, unfortunately, often in our homes.

I wonder what it would mean for trans people if our powerful opposition were brought down from their thrones. I wonder what it would mean for everyone else if trans people were lifted up as an example of living authentically in the face of great difficulty. I wonder if each of us, you and I, can join with Mary and all advocates and activists for gender justice throughout history and around the world to help to improve the lives of all people, trans or not. Could you be a part of God's mission for justice?

Prayer:

He has brought down the powerful from their thrones,
  and lifted up the lowly;
he has filled the hungry with good things,
  and sent the rich away empty.

God of justice, sometimes we look up and wonder –
will you also bring down those who hold on to power and control today?

God of the margins, sometimes we look around us and wonder –
will you also lift up those who are oppressed today?

God our parent, feed us –
with your hunger for justice.
Amen

Action:

Consider visiting www.transgenderchristianhuman.com to find out how we are campaigning for justice, and see if you feel called to join in.

Alex Clare-Young

Third Week of Advent, Monday

Bible reading:

Finally, be strong in the Lord and in the strength of his power. Put on the whole armour of God, so that you may be able to stand against the wiles of the devil.

Ephesians 6:10–11 (NRSV)

Reflection:

After the Bible, John Bunyan's *Pilgrim's Progress* (1678) is the most published book in the English language. An allegory of the Christian life as a journey to God, one of the most vivid scenes in the book is when the protagonist, Christian, battles Apollyon (Rev 9:11) in the Valley of Humiliation. Prior to reaching the valley, Christian stayed at the House Beautiful, a rest stop for pilgrims, where he was equipped with armour from head to foot in case he should '*meet with assaults in the way*'.

While walking through the Valley of Humiliation, Christian saw Apollyon crossing the field towards him. Christian debated whether he should retreat or stand his ground – and we are left wondering what Christian will do, until Bunyan provides a key detail regarding his allegorical interpretation of the armour of God. Though covered in front from head to foot, Christian has no armour on his back. The point of spiritual armour, Bunyan implies, is to confront the enemy head-on – not to run away, exposing our weakness as we flee. And so, Christian stood his ground, facing battle with Apollyon. Dramatic banter, flaming darts and pitched battle ensued for the better part of a day. Though weary and wounded and almost pressed to death, Christian, at last, wounds Apollyon with a fatal thrust of his sword ('*the word of God*'): '*in all these things we are more than conquerors through [God] that loved us*' (Rom 8:37).

If *Pilgrim's Progress* turns the Bible into an allegory of the Christian journey to God, its secondary metaphor is '*life is a battle*'. The martial images may not always resonate with our modern-day sensibilities; yet, we can hardly blame John Bunyan, given scriptures like Ephesians 6. The earthly life is treacherous; evil lurks in open daylight. Preparedness is imperative. So, too, is not underestimating the enemy. Ephesians 6 respects the prowess of the evil one while asserting the ultimate strength of a God-focused, God-infused faith.

John Bunyan holds that God's armour is not simply for defensive purposes. To stand firm is to face life going forward. Abundant life is faith full-on. The imitation of Christ is a 'no retreat' journey.

Life presents us, at times, with difficult options: the path forward seems irredeemably obstructed, while fleeing only exposes our backside.

Paul's imagery of the armour of God is a word picture that we are not left to fend for ourselves. We are surrounded, supplied, equipped and empowered by an unconquerable universal power whose name is love. That does not mean that life is without its battles. Christian struggled with Apollyon for hours; the Advent journey takes us through the darkest days of the year; armour is given, because armour will be used. Yet, in the midst of the Valley of Humiliation, God delivers us from the evil one; light shines in the darkness, and equipped with the shield of faith and the helmet of salvation, God's people stand firm. Wounds are healed, and life wins. Cosmic powers are defeated as, together with Christian, we continue on our journey towards the Celestial City.

The valiant man by handling Sword and Shield,
Doth make him, tho' a Dragon, quit the field.

Words for reflection:

Vulnerabilities, Fears, Protection, and Strength
Standing Firm, Face-Front Battles, Empowered by God
Faith, Perseverance, Victory in Jesus …

Great Beelzebub, the captain of this fiend,
Design'd my ruin; therefore to this end
He sent him harness'd out, and he with rage

That hellish was, did fiercely me engage.
But blessed Michael helped me, and I,
By dint of sword did quickly make him fly.
Therefore to him let me give lasting praise,
And thanks, and bless his holy name always!

Christian's reflection on his battle with Apollyon, *Pilgrim's Progress*

Rodney Aist

Third Week of Advent, Tuesday

Bible reading:

Those who trust in the Lord are like Mount Zion,
*   which cannot be moved, but abides forever.*
As the mountains surround Jerusalem,
*   so the Lord surrounds his people*
*   from this time on and forevermore.*

Psalm 125:1–2 (NRSV)

Reflection:

We live in a fast-moving world; a world where you can pick and choose between things and people as easily as you can swipe up or down, left or right on your mobile phone. With avatars and carefully edited personal profiles, the potential for fake news and scams, it can be increasingly difficult to know who to trust and what to trust. Data and statistics can be manipulated, recordings can be seamlessly altered and holiday snaps can be filtered to tell one story rather than another.

Not knowing what or who to trust is like trying to walk on shifting sands. As a result, we can be tempted to rely on our own resources, to trust in our own capacity to lay down a solid foundation from which to step out and engage life. We place our hope in what we can acquire and construct to protect us and keep us secure. However, deep down, a fear can remain that this edifice could, like a sandcastle, dissolve under the scouring impact and force of any approaching tide.

Threat and menace for some is both a fear and a present reality. It comes in the ferocious attacks of war, poverty and disease; evils that engulf lives with an overwhelming daily bombardment of hardship and torment. The land beneath the feet of those who suffer quivers in the wake of the latest shelling, rumbles through the empty bellies of children and vibrates to the grief of pain and mourning.

Trouble has always lurked in the wings through every age for every people. The pilgrims made their ascent to Jerusalem looking up at Mount Zion and sang of the sceptre of the wicked over the land as they progressed. They could quell their fear by simply seeking peace with whatever threatened them and by turning away from God to stand on a sandy compromise with evil; or they could anchor themselves in God's presence and the assurance that his protection and care surrounded them just as the mountains visibly surrounded Jerusalem.

They could place their trust in the Lord. To do so was not simply to move from shaky ground to solid ground, it was to become like the very rock itself in its resistance, strength and permanence. To do so was to become like the mountains; like Mount Zion.

Trusting in the Lord does not remove the threats that are out there; it does not of itself solve the problems of the debt collector at the door or the cyber bully on the screen but it draws round us the comfort and consolation of the presence of the Lord, which then lays down beneath us a foundation from which to persevere and not lose hope regardless of our circumstances.

These verses invite us to picture ourselves standing on Mount Zion taking in the 360 degree view of the hills that surround Jerusalem so that we can also understand that to trust in the Lord fully encircles us with a presence that is constant, enduring and reliable; a high barricade against the source of our fear.

For the pilgrims ascending to Jerusalem, Mount Zion was the centre, the place where Isaiah declared Yahweh dwelt and reigned. For us, Jesus is the centre and he said he is with us always, to the end of the age; a promise fulfilled in the gift of his Holy Spirit which confirms his abiding presence with each one of us.

Therefore, we can trust and be confident that, whatever the evil that threatens us, as we turn to God, he will strengthen and enable us to stand firm by the power of his Holy Spirit, he will fortify us with the living hope of his resurrected Son and he will surround us with his everlasting love as Father today, tomorrow and every day evermore.

Action:

Find a rock or stone, and as you hold it in your hand, reflect on Romans 8:38–39:

For I am convinced that neither death, nor life, nor angels, nor rulers, nor things present, nor things to come, nor powers, nor height, nor depth, nor anything else in all creation, will be able to separate us from the love of God in Christ Jesus our Lord. (NRSV)

Sarah Dickinson

Third Week of Advent, Wednesday

Bible reading:

Those who trust in the Lord are like Mount Zion,
which cannot be moved, but abides for ever.

Psalm 125:1 (NRSV)

Reflection:

Christianity has always been big on beliefs, and falling out over them. At a Church version of the European Union, in Nicaea in AD 325, a treaty called the Nicene Creed was settled on. That one, or a slightly different one, the Apostles' Creed, is still recited in many churches today. Both are full of answers to questions people were asking 1,700 years ago.

Depending on your answers, you are in.

Or out.

In the twenty-first century, the great faith traditions are caught up in a long-running argument over what their adherents believe. We hear about people of faith, not because of what they do, but because of what they believe. Or don't. Do women have the same rights as men? Are LGBT people affirmed? Or ostracised? Do the findings of science contradict religion? Or complement it? Is a holy book prescriptive? Or for general guidance?

The Church has taught that if we can get our beliefs right then we'll be able to get our actions right. Orthodoxy leads to orthopraxis. Otherwise there will be weeping and gnashing of teeth, which will require orthodontistry. While religion often oversells doctrine it often undersells community and friendship. Theologian Ann Morisy noticed that Jesus didn't say 'I speak the way', or, 'I believe the way'. He said: 'I am the way.' He didn't say 'I'll speak true words to you', or, 'I'll tell you about the truth', but 'I am the truth'.[1]

He saw truth in relationships and friendship, not in facts and dogma. If you wanted to know truth you needed to become friends, and the community of those friends eventually got called 'Church'. It was a circle of trust – trusting God, trusting each other. More personal, less doctrinal.

Theologian Marcus Borg noticed that over the centuries the meaning of the word 'belief' has changed. Before 1600, the verb 'believe' always had a person as its direct object. It did not mean believing that a statement (say, 'I believe in the Virgin Birth') is true, but more like what we mean when we say to somebody: 'I believe in you.'

To believe in somebody, said Borg, is not the same as believing somebody. 'I believe in you' means I have confidence in you. For people of faith that means having confidence in God.

The Old English *be loef* is the root of the word believe and it means 'to hold dear', and is related to the word 'belove'. Originally the etymology of belief was about trust, but somewhere down the line, the trust element was displaced in favour of the 'mental assertion of an extremely long list of facts' element. In favour of insiders versus outsiders. Those who can sign up to every line of a creed … and those who can't.

Actually, said Borg, the Latin root of the word credo – from which we get the word creed – means 'I give my heart to'. 'Heart,' he said, 'is a metaphor for the self at its deepest level – a level of the self beneath our thinking, willing and feeling.'[2]

'Do you believe in me?' meant 'Do you belove me?'

In the end beliefs are often overrated. There is only one article of faith. Love.

The earliest Christians, keeping the story of Jesus alive when it was difficult and dangerous, famously made drawings on the walls of catacombs. Sending messages to one another. Simple reminders that we can trust God. An anchor, because we can be tethered to God in the roughest seas. Someone carrying a sheep over their shoulders – because we can rely on a Good Shepherd. A ship in rocky seas, because God will bring us to safe harbour. Solid ground. Terra firma.

As the Psalmist puts it, *'Those who trust in the Lord are like Mount Zion, which cannot be moved, but abides forever.'*

Martin Wroe

Notes:

1. See *Journeying Out: A New Approach to Christian Mission*, Ann Morisy, Continuum, 2004

2. See *Speaking Christian: Recovering the Lost Meaning of Christian Words*, Marcus J Borg, SPCK, 2011

Third Week of Advent, Thursday

Bible reading:

He is the reflection of God's glory and the exact imprint of God's very being ...

Hebrews 1:3a (NRSV)

Reflection:

Reading through the Book of Hebrews got me thinking about glory. This book is filled with images of angels, priests and sacrifices offering glory to God. Soon music for Christmas will fill the air with glorias, and the glory of the Lord will shine on certain shepherds. Hebrews' word for 'glory', transliterated *doxa*, meant 'opinion' in ancient Greek, but Hebrews is not asking us for our opinions about God, as happy as we might be to share them. No, ancient believers understood *doxa*, glory, to be part of God's nature, the radiance of God's very being. To give God glory was to reflect back the glory already encountered flowing out from God. Giving glory was not expressing an opinion about God, but rather embracing God who has already embraced us.

How do you think about glory? When have you experienced glory? I first thought of stepping out into a 'glorious day', breathing in a moment of nature's beauty ... combined with well-behaved weather, watching rich colours of sunset bloom on a lovely evening or enjoying stars dancing in a clear night sky. Then I recalled 'glorious music', performances that overwhelmed me in their resonance, leaving me breathless, sensing applause would spoil the glory. Consider when you have met glory and the features of your experience. Glory seems always to have embraced me first, drawing my response of wonder.

My experience helps me appreciate the ancient view of God's glory, radiating out to us, enveloping us in God's holy wonder. Experiencing glory in nature's beauty and in amazing music connects me with God's creative power, provoking spontaneous prayer of adoration and gratitude. Glory invites glorifying – which brings me back to the Book of Hebrews.

Today's phrase for contemplation calls Christ the 'reflection' or 'radiance' of God's glory, the One who expresses *'God's very being'*. Many images in the rest of this book echo the splendours of temples and altars, high and holy. Yet as our celebrations of the Nativity approach, we will focus on the infant Jesus wearing the new face of God's glory in a more mundane setting.

On a recent trip to Sicily, I saw a painting of the Nativity scene by Caravaggio, in which the artist's trademark shaft of light beams on mother and child in a way that left me breathless. I was sure that if I touched the canvas, the infant's skin would be warm to my touch. That's the new face of God's glory radiating from Christ, glory we can touch, which responds to our touch.

Think about God's glory snuggling in his mother's arms, exchanging warmth and tenderness. That glory continues to reach out to us, teaching and touching eager souls; laughing, eating, arguing at table with odds and sods of followers; waiting, weeping, bruised and bleeding, agonising and dying, radiating God's love into our lives. God's glory reaches out to embrace us. And Hebrews calls for our response to this new face of God's glory. It invites us to reflect back this passionate glory in the ways we teach and learn, in the hospitality we share, in agonising and rejoicing together, because we are embracing the One who has embraced us from cradle to cross – and beyond.

As this Advent season flows toward Christmas, listen for carols crying 'Glory!', inviting us to respond with our own 'Glorias'. We give glory to God in the highest because, in Christ, the glory of God has found us right here. To that I will add a breathless 'Alleluia!' this year.

Prayer:

Holy, holy, holy, God of mystery and mercy!
Glory to you for your creative love
which we meet in breathtaking beauty,
moving music,
exhilarating exertion,
surprised silence.

Holy, holy, holy, God of manger and main street!
Glory to you for your tender touch
which we meet in Christ Jesus,
reaching out to embrace us, whoever we are,
walking with us, whatever we face,
challenging us with healing and hope.

Turn our cries of Glory into glorious acts
for justice and joy,
touching lives with the healing and hope we have met in Christ Jesus,
from cradle to cross,
who shows us your true Glory in his undying love.

Nancy Cocks

Third Week of Advent, Friday

Bible reading:

For to which of the angels did God ever say,

> *'You are my Son;*
>> *today I have begotten you'? …*

Of the angels he says,

> *'He makes his angels winds,*
>> *and his servants flames of fire.'*

But of the Son he says,

> *'Your throne, O God, is forever and ever,*
>> *and the righteous sceptre is the sceptre of your kingdom.' …*

But to which of the angels has he ever said,

> *'Sit at my right hand*
>> *until I make your enemies a footstool for your feet'?*

Are not all angels spirits in the divine service, sent to serve for the sake of those who are to inherit?

Hebrews 1:5,7–8,13–14 (NRSV)

Reflection:

Have you ever dreamed that you can fly? No, I don't mean at 30,000 feet strapped in a sardine can with two hundred others, but hovering above the earth, or rising up high like an eagle. It's a common dream, to have the freedom to go where you like in three dimensions, like a bird not bound to the earth, which is our natural state. This wonder at the freedom of birds to go where they like is surely the root of the traditional picture of the angels of heaven, who wait upon God to do his bidding.

Christmas is a time for angels, and it is not difficult for us to imagine the multitude of the heavenly host singing Glory to the shepherds watching their flocks by night on the hills outside Bethlehem. The writer of Hebrews clearly has these heavenly beings in mind in the opening chapter of his letter. In a series of essays or sermons his purpose is to take key passages from the Old Testament, and to interpret them in order to show the superiority of Jesus the Christ as High Priest, as mediator of the New Covenant; and the sacrifice of Jesus on the cross as superior to the sacrificial system based on temple worship. Wonderful as these angelic beings are, their glory is eclipsed by that of the Son, who is superior in every way.

But there is another picture of angels given to us in Hebrews that is altogether different. No golden harps, no shining wings. These are simply messengers of God who come in ordinary human form. One must presume that is the case, because their appearance is not remarked upon. What is important is the message, not the messenger; like the three who visited Abraham and Sarah to tell them of the coming birth of their child in their old age. It is this tradition that the writer of Hebrews uses near the end of his letter when he is listing practical instructions for leading a Christian life: *'Do not neglect to show hospitality to strangers, for by doing that some have entertained angels without knowing it'* (Heb 13:2, NRSV).

It is this tradition that Jesus applies to himself in Matthew 25: *'Lord, when did we see you hungry, or thirsty, or sick, or in prison and did (or did not) come to your aid?'* – Christ in the guise of the poor, the foreigner, the discriminated against. The One who died an outcast, enduring a criminal's death, is the One for whom there was no room at the inn (Luke), and who became a refugee with his family (Matthew). This is the One who is our Saviour, if we welcome him in the guise of the homeless refugee and the outsider this Christmas, and throughout the year.

Bob Rhodes

Angels

I can't picture God.
I have no clue to what She looks like;
just a sense of something there, to which I pray.

Christ I can imagine,
though not the pale-skinned Jesus of my childhood
feeding lambs; my Christ quite different.

The Holy Spirit – Wild Goose, wind and wave.

But angels – those I *do* know something of;
not the dolly ones, with papery wings and painted faces
balancing on tops of Christmas trees,
or even Fra Angelico's gentle agent –
though he comes closer.

No, but the man who shared my bereavement story
on a train, the asylum seeker who showed me life
beyond myself, the young woman
who opened a wider world to me,
teaching me empathy,
and warm eyes above a mask.

They are but messengers, interpreters,
not gods, but those of spirit
conveying the best of all we can receive
when least expected:
the love of God.

Jill Rhodes

Third Week of Advent, Saturday

Bible reading:

When they heard these words, some in the crowd said, 'This is really the prophet.' Others said, 'This is the Messiah.' But some asked, 'Surely the Messiah does not come from Galilee, does he? Has not the scripture said that the Messiah is descended from David and comes from Bethlehem, the village where David lived?' So there was a division in the crowd because of him. Some of them wanted to arrest him, but no one laid hands on him.

John 7:40–44 (NRSV)

Reflection:

You can't blame people for doubting that Jesus was the Messiah; he simply didn't fit the criteria. The Messiah would be a descendant of David, born in Bethlehem, who would free Judea from its enemies and reign in Jerusalem. Obviously that meant raising an army against the Romans. A wandering preacher from Galilee just didn't fit the bill.

And yet ... there was that about him which made you wonder – made you doubt all those confident preconceptions about what you should expect the Messiah to be like; something which made even some Pharisees think that maybe they should wait and see where all this was going.

Jesus' disciples firmly believed that he was the Messiah, but even they hung on to the preconception of reigning in Jerusalem. 'Can we be your chief ministers?' (James and John); 'Stop talking about being killed; that just isn't going to happen' (Peter). And some have suggested that Judas' betrayal of Jesus was an attempt to force him to declare himself and lead the people in revolution.

What are our preconceptions as we live out our faith in C21 of the Christian era? What assumptions do we bring to our striving for peace, justice and the integrity of creation?

A couple of examples.

'The powerful don't care about people disadvantaged by their policies.'

I worked with Labour and Conservative ministers in my career as a civil servant. All those I knew well truly believed that the policies they were implementing would make life better for all of us. Sometimes they were right, sometimes not; but when they were wrong, it was because the left- or right-wing academic theory, which they passionately believed would work, did not stand up to contact with the unpredictability of real life.

Of course there are some powerful people who are only interested in their own status and career, but we should not start by assuming that the person whose policies or actions we are campaigning against is one of them.

'People in poverty are in that position because they are lazy.'

Politicians and much of the media tell us that if only people would try hard and do the right thing, they would not need to rely on the state. But Covid-19 has shown dramatically what has always been true – that people who are managing OK by working hard at a low-paid job have no financial resilience to meet a major shock like being made redundant or being forced by circumstance to stop working. The thousands of people who have claimed Universal Credit since the pandemic struck are no different from the vast majority of those who were already claiming.

There are some people who are cheating the system, and the TV programmes focus on them. But most people in poverty want nothing more than a job at a decent wage which allows them to pay their way.

As it happens, these are not my preconceptions; I could not write this if they were – but I do have my own different preconceptions, and need to ask myself how open I am to questioning them.

It is important to challenge those preconceptions we see in others, but in these last few days of Advent, let's start with ourselves.

When I have understood and challenged my own preconceptions, I will be better able to challenge the assumptions our society makes which lead to a failure of peace, justice and the integrity of creation.

As we approach our celebration of the Bethlehem birth of the Messiah from Galilee, let us challenge our own ingrained preconceptions about other people in the light of the Iona Community's affirmation of *'God's goodness at the heart of humanity, planted more deeply than all that is wrong'*.

Action:

Each day from now until Christmas Day, think about a person or a group of people whose statements and actions make you angry. It may be a long-standing issue or something you read in the news that day. Identify and challenge your preconceptions about them and pray for them, yourself and the issue involved, that all may live and act in the light of God's goodness planted in their heart.

Alison Jackson

Fourth Sunday of Advent

Bible reading:

And Mary said,

'My soul magnifies the Lord,
and my spirit rejoices in God my Saviour,
for he has looked with favour on the lowliness of his servant.
Surely, from now on all generations will call me blessed;
for the Mighty One has done great things for me,
and holy is his name.'

Luke 1:46–55 (NRSV)

Reflection:

In a few days, the world will again celebrate the birth of Christ, but on this fourth Sunday in Advent let us not think of that celebration only in our own home and locality. Awaken your imagination to help you sit beside our sisters and brothers in many parts of the world, who are living in abject poverty, in the shadows of war, in the reality of racial injustice, in abusive relationships, in the prison of a tortured mind. Millions of people, with whom we share a common heartbeat, are in such situations as we read these words in Luke's Gospel. They may be far off or next door.

This beautifully poetic utterance, placed on the lips of a very young woman soon to give birth, has, for centuries, touched the hearts of Christians and of those who seek spiritual meaning in their lives. And in that long span of human history biblical scholars around the globe have been analysing Mary's song and searching for its multiple meanings. One of these scholars, G.W.H. Lampe, made the point that many of the words attributed to Mary in the Magnificat look back to the Song of Hannah in the Book of Samuel, and to certain of the great Psalms.

Mary's challenging song of awakening links the fulfilment of the Messianic hope of Israel with the original promise to Abraham. That promise is being made not through those in power, but through the hidden life of a young woman in a remote part of the Roman Empire. It is one of the hidden people of our human story who carries the Messiah, and that humble spirit rejoices in that extraordinary truth. In this instance, God certainly has given a body swerve to the rich, corrupt and powerful and as the gospel succinctly puts it *'has lifted up the lowly'*. Or to say it differently, the 'forgotten' are definitely within the heart of God, actively turning our hearts of stone to risk-taking tenderness.

It is for this reason that I think Mary's words have such resonance in our time, when dictatorships are again realities, when the rich are being given permission by their leaders to tramp, literally and metaphorically, on the poor, and when the word 'lockdown' has become commonplace. Who among us in these strange times when fear stalks our streets wants to concentrate their attention on the abandoned and oppressed? Certainly some great souls do, but the reality that gives us all hope is that the One who holds this world in his or her hands certainly does. That is the soul-making truth which lies at the heart of the Magnificat. It is a glorious affirmation about the hidden ones of the earth, propelling us all to emerge from our bunkers and walk in solidarity and love with those in the shadows. It is an invitation to be again amazed by the kind of people God is constantly inviting to his banquets.

You are not hidden, Mary, nor are all our sisters and brothers who today are on the streets of the world asking their leaders that they too may have a place in the sun. All these years ago, the Lord of Israel made a promise to the people, but in these weeks of Advent we again affirm that this same promise is alive and well for the world today. At the core of that promise is the belief that however tough the journey, the hidden ones will experience both justice and liberation.

As Dr Martin Luther King said: *Our lives begin to end the day we become silent about things that matter.* Mary's words remind us of many things that matter, not least that all the 'hidden ones' of human history matter a great deal to God.

Prayer:

Thank you, Lord,
for the mystery, beauty and challenge
embedded in today's gospel message.
Thank you for Mary and for all 'ordinary folk',
who matter so much to the One
who loves us all.

Peter Millar

Fourth Week of Advent, Monday

Bible reading:

And Mary sang, 'God gets bigger and bigger in me.'

Luke 1:46a (from my remembered Bible)

Reflection:

There's a lot of violence in the Bible. Violent death is at the heart of the Christian faith. But so, according to some commentators, is violent conception.

Mary has a song to sing and she sings it out as loudly as possible, and we keep repeating it.

Mary certainly sings, but much remains unsung. Some biblical commentators have suggested that Mary was a survivor of sexual violence. It makes sense to me. Galilee was occupied by the Roman army and Mary was a teenager who got pregnant. Ask any woman who lives in an occupied country what can happen that may be silenced and you may catch a whisper of Mary's story. It doesn't even have to be an occupied country; any kind of lockdown will do.

And what if we add the voices of the foremothers (as in Matthew chapter 1)? Mary had a whole load of foremothers who also survived sexual violence.

The stories in the Bible are open to interpretation of course. But in the light of the 'Me Too movement' (#MeToo) and several decades of feminist biblical scholarship, it seems to me that:

Tamar tried to make the best of a bad situation – dead husband, brother-in-law 'spilling seed', so she got pregnant by Judah, who then threatened to get rid of her.

Rahab is the one with the most silence – she gets out of Jericho on the back of helping the spies but we don't know how she became a sex worker. (I recently read a memoir of an immigrant to the U.S. who had to do sex work.)

It was a women's officer at the WCC whom I first heard suggest that Naomi had trafficked Ruth. This is tricky if you always thought Ruth and Naomi were buddies. But many others have suggested this. Naomi tells Ruth, '*Sleep at his feet*', i.e. have sex with Boaz.

Bathsheba isn't even given a name at first. David is a voyeur, and then has her husband murdered, then marries her and later her baby dies.

It's all pretty desperate stuff.

To make Mary the Mother of God into an icon without the red stain, without the red thread or rope, is to miss something, and to silence them all again.

And rape, abuse, trafficking, sex slavery, incest still happen.

In many communities the Magnificat is sung daily. For me it is a battle cry. Mary still sings, and we can sing with her.

Here is a version of Mary's song I caught a whisper of in 2020:

In this song I make God bigger and bigger.
Everyone is amazed at what God has done for me,
the lowest of the low, no longer a maiden.
But God's blessing will surely scupper the rumours,
for whatever else is true, God is holy,
and every generation fears God.

The army of occupation fears no one;
it takes what it wants from women lying on their backs in the dirt.
In a land, far from home, men do what they want.
They take us like possessions, overpowering us,
and we are not strong enough to resist.
Though we are too weak to stop them, God's arm is strong.

As each belly grows bigger, so does our resistance:
so God gets bigger in each one of us.
An army may seem powerful, but it cannot last forever:
armies will be scattered and eventually bought down.

This empire may rule the land now
but one day it will come to an end
and the lowly will take over.

We may be hungry now but it will not always be like this.
We will survive: justice will be delivered.
You have heard all the stories;
you know how my foremothers overcame
the violence that had been done against them.
We will have many descendants,
and my own child will take his place before you all.
Not proudly, but humbly, he will be lifted up,
so that all will take the knee before him,
thankful for God's deliverance.
I can hold on to God's promises and pass these words on
from one generation to another.
I who am called full, am also empty;
I am called to be nothing but also everything.
It's a tough challenge, but I say yes to God
and it's what God does that counts.

And you might want to sing this too:

(Tune: 'O Tannenbaum')

The old red rag is hanging here;
it is a sign we hold no fear.
We've been abused, raped and defiled;
our silent stories were reviled.
But now we raise our song again,
so you may know we've come through pain;
that each voice here will make it clear:
We'll keep the red rag flying here.

Janet Lees

Fourth Week of Advent, Tuesday

Bible reading:

He has brought down the powerful from their thrones,
    and lifted up the lowly;
he has filled the hungry with good things,
    and sent the rich away empty.

Luke 1:52–53 (NRSV)

I'm sitting in a community centre next to the primary school, watching people from the local estate coming in to pick up their veg bags. Someone's giving out cake and tea; on the side some older residents are enjoying watching the children play, and parents, mostly mothers, greet and swap gossip. It's lively, noisy, busy and great fun. It's also a food lifeline: this is a food-buying co-operative, since the only local shop has very limited fresh produce, and a small bunch of determined women, all lone mothers, have created a good alternative system. Co-op members put in a weekly list, the women sort out what everyone wants and go off very early to buy it from a wholesaler (rare, these days), and spend the morning bagging up the orders. Then everyone collects and pays, and there's always extra for those who want it. People spend what they can, they try new things, they exchange recipes, and everyone is filled with good things – healthy food which nourishes body, mind and soul, pleasure in a market and from cooking. No one is eating leftovers or end-of-line/nearly out of date stuff donated in charity, and no one is feeling anxious or inadequate. Yet everyone here counts as poor in the UK, and many would otherwise be hungry. They are also showing the corporate companies and power-brokers who say they are economically dead and socially worthless that they are absolutely neither.

I was there, some 20 years ago, to find out what made local food projects 'work'. The key things, perhaps unsurprisingly, were community ownership and a modest but secure funding stream. Of course, what also made this food co-operative work, where normal retail said it couldn't survive, was a peppercorn rent, endless free labour and total commitment from the volunteers, who had worked out that 'good food' is more than calories and nutrients – it's the glue of community life and the key to human flourishing. And they saw that these were for the poor too. Sharing hospitality, pleasure in food – and we might add rich pastures, good husbandry, teeming nets and clean flowing water – are the markers of a thriving food system. Throughout the Bible these are signs of God's generous creativity and love, which is for everyone.

Two decades on, I know that many community-led initiatives in areas of deprivation, in the UK and elsewhere, are struggling to survive from long-term austerity policies which have driven down people's hopes and taken their time and energy. Covid-19 has mostly made things harder still. There's now a desperate desire to move on from 'emergency feeding' to building resilience for the problems – political, economic, environmental – we know are ahead. Some are optimistic but many fear things will get much worse.

Mary's song, the extraordinary celebration of revolutionary reversals, is so marvellous and familiar – who could not rejoice that the powerful might be brought down and the lowly lifted up, that the hungry be filled with good things (not just be kept alive, told to be grateful). How we long for these changes to come!

And yet, the rich [he] sent away empty. How stark, and how unlike our loving God – to send people away, unfilled. I find these the most challenging of words, in this Advent season of anticipation and judgement. I am rich (I don't feel it, but I am, in material fact) and I live in a rich country. I try to be aware of my debt to so many others, past and present, whose harsh and unfulfilled lives mean that I have a comfortable life – with warmth, good clothing and food, leisure to meet friends, travel and enjoy the arts and new places. The reality is that I too readily take all I have for granted. I think I deserve it. I don't give enough away or share with those who really need the basics and more. Jesus said it was pretty hard for a rich person to enter the kingdom of heaven. Mary's song challenges me to recognise what a long way I have to go.

Prayer:

Lord, open our eyes to our place in the order of things.

Challenge our lack of awareness where our lives depend on systems that exploit and are unjust.

Forgive our complacency; give us grace and courage to engage in reflection and action to bring about change.

Help us avoid the thinking which says that there isn't enough to go round, so some must have less, when in fact, in your abundance, there is plenty for everyone's needs.

Liz Dowler

Fourth Week of Advent, Wednesday

Bible reading:

And Mary said:

My soul magnifies YHWH
and my spirit rejoices in God my Saviour,
for he has regarded the low estate of his maid servant …

He has scattered the proud in the imagination of their hearts;
the mighty he has toppled from their thrones,
and exalted those of low degree.

Luke 1:46–47, 51–52

Luke, the foremost artist in the Messianic writings (not for nothing is he the patron saint of painters), begins his story with a pastiche formed of phrases and themes from the Hebrew Bible. The girl Merriam conceives and Luke puts a psalm in her mouth, loosely based on the Song of Hannah in 1 Samuel. In Hannah's song the emphasis is on G-d's overruling of all history; in Merriam's song it is on what G-d is doing through this particular birth. Both songs celebrate the fact that G-d raises the poor and needy and humbles the proud (1 Sam 2:4).

There are plenty of stories about strong rulers in the Hebrew Bible, and plenty of dreams of imperial glory, but there is also, in Isaiah, the uniquely powerful development of the Servant theme. We have every reason to believe that Reb Joshua ruminated on this theme profoundly. In fact, it informed his understanding both of G-d, and of his own vocation. G-d, he was convinced, worked not through the so-called 'great men' of history, but through solidarity and service. All four evangelists make this clear and Luke artfully makes it underpin his birth story. The Song of Merriam is a great cry of exultation that G-d has made an *'option for the poor'*.

G-d has scattered the proud and put down the mighty from their thrones. Really? Where exactly do we see this? Is there any cathedral which celebrates this? Who do the monuments which fill them commemorate? Mostly they commemorate the powerful, showing that they have not heard or understood Reb Joshua's ruminations. As a kind of mockery the Song of Merriam is given ornate settings to make sure its message is not heard. If we do hear it, though, what follows for our economy, our politics, our social structure? Donald Reeves, at St James' Piccadilly, spelled some of this out in his prayer for the breaking of bread at the Eucharist:

We break this bread for those who follow other paths:
for those who follow the noble path of the Buddha,
the yogic path of the Hindus,
the way of the Eternal Guru of the Sikhs,
and for the other children of Abraham, the Jews,
from whom Jesus came,
and for our neighbours the Muslims.
We welcome to this table
the wisdom of other traditions
and we seek to open our hearts to that wisdom
as we seek the courage, the strength and the humility
to share the wisdom and truth that we know in Jesus.

We break this bread for the broken earth,
ravaged and plundered for greed.
And we welcome to this table
the wisdom of the indigenous peoples of the world
who too have suffered because of their love and care for the earth.
We seek to open our hearts to their wisdom for our times.

We break this bread for our broken humanity,
for the powerful and the powerless trapped by exploitation and oppression.
And we welcome to this table
the rich and the poor,

the ignored and the influential,
for we seek to sing Mary's song
where the poor are raised up and the rich brought low
to stand together in the reign of God.

We break this bread for our broken selves,
for the unhealed hurts and wounds that lie within us all,
and we welcome to this table
our feelings of doubt and confusion,
our feelings of hopelessness and despair,
our feelings of violence and hatred,
for we seek to know God's love,
healing and forgiveness
and Christ's resurrection joy.

Donald Reeves[1]

Tim Gorringe

Note:

1. Used with permission

Christmas Eve

Bible reading:

And she gave birth to her firstborn son and wrapped him in bands of cloth, and laid him in a manger, because there was no place for them in the inn.

… When they saw this, they made known what had been told them about this child; and all who heard it were amazed at what the shepherds told them.

Luke 2:7, 17–18 (NRSV)

Reflection: Miracle

It was a miracle.
A miracle that Joseph stuck with the girl he was engaged to
when he realised she was carrying a child that was not his.
A miracle that the first ever Roman census drove them to Bethlehem,
and that when they could not find anywhere to stay there
someone offered them a stable.
It was definitely a miracle that the baby was delivered safely,
after such a journey, in such conditions,
that very night.
A miracle, as well, that a random group of hillside shepherds,
total strangers to everyone,
turned up with an unlikely tale
that made sense of it all;
that they had managed to find their way there in fact.
And a miracle that all these things coincided the way they did.

But then, every birth is a miracle.
Relationships, journeys, shelter, stories,
survival against the odds,
people finding their way,
things coinciding …
they are all miracles.
Life itself is a miracle!

Ah – but at the centre of this story
(at the centre of everything, some would say)
was the miracle of miracles –
that the people in the stable
looked at that little scrap of humanity,
all wrapped up in cloths and rags,
and saw God!

Child of the night,
you who one day would open the eyes of the blind;
and who people would call Son of God:
open my eyes, too,
till I start to see in everyone, everything,
what those in the stable saw in you.

Open my eyes
to see the holiness of every birth,
and God in every living person,
made in God's image,
loved as God's child.
Open my eyes to see God
in friend and stranger;
in unlikely story and unexpected happening;
in the world that God loves;
in this fragile planet;
in the whole created universe.
And, though I can scarcely believe it could be so,
help me to find God deep in myself.

Child of the night,
open my eyes to this God who is beyond imagination,
yet comes close;
open my life to miracle.

Brian Woodcock

Christmas Day

Bible reading:

And the Word became flesh and lived among us, and we have seen his glory,
the glory as of a father's only son, full of grace and truth.

John 1:14 (NRSV)

Reflection:

In many churches the Prologue of John's Gospel is the traditional reading
for Christmas Day. It is possible that the Prologue is based on an early
Christian hymn (cf. Phil 2:6–11; Col 1:15–20). The poetic language of the
Prologue invites us to reflect on Christ and his relationship to the world.

The first five verses have a cosmological focus which explore the relationship between Christ and creation. The opening verse echoes the start of
the Book of Genesis: '*In the beginning …*' Jesus is identified with the Word
of God which is present with God at the beginning of creation. All things
come into being through the Word, and Jesus is identified with life and
light. In Genesis, God separates light from darkness but in John's Gospel
there is a suggestion of a struggle between light and darkness. Darkness
appears to be a force which opposes God. Light entered a dark world, but
the darkness did not '*overcome*' the light (Jn 1:5).

Verses 6–8 introduce the historical figure of John the Baptist, who acts as
a witness to Jesus. These verses are written in prose, and may be an
addition to the original hymn. Verses 9–13 describe the impact of the
coming of light into the world. They express the mystery that the world
was created through the Word but did not recognise him. The Word is
rejected by some but accepted by others who believe in his name. These
people receive power to become the '*children of God*'.

The most startling verse in the Prologue is verse 14, which states that '*the*
Word became flesh'. This verse would have been shocking to early Christians. In the Greco-Roman world the realm of the spirit and the realm of

the flesh are regarded as incompatible. God is eternal, transcendent and remote from earthly existence. There is a gulf between God and humanity, and between the spiritual realm and the material realm. In the Prologue, the Word crosses these boundaries, and 'becomes' flesh. The Greek term *sarx* (flesh) refers to the transitory sphere of life which is subject to decay and death. Christ shares in the constraints and the messiness of human life.

In the Prologue we see a tension between images of strength and images of vulnerability. There is a contrast between images of power and invincibility and images of fragility. Jesus is the Word of God, and he is life and light. Yet he is also the Word which becomes '*flesh*'. The world came into being through him, but he lives in the world unrecognised. There is a vulnerability in the account of the Word becoming flesh, since some people reject the Word but some people do see the glory of God in the flesh.

John 1:14b bears witness to the experience of the community of faith. The use of '*we*' refers to the experience of those who have seen Jesus. The reference to '*glory*' alludes to the power and presence of God. In the Old Testament the 'glory' of God is associated with magnificence, splendour and light. The prophet Isaiah is blinded by the dazzling glory of God in the Temple (Is 6:1–5). In the Prologue, however, not all human beings recognise the glory of God in Jesus. How do we glimpse the divine glory in the flesh? Jesus is not a divine being who is merely concealed by the flesh. He does not live apart from the suffering of the world. He 'becomes' a human being subject to the same emotions, hopes and fears.

In the Prologue the community bears witness that it is possible to see the glory of God in the humanity of Jesus. Jesus lives among us as one of us, and he lives a life '*full of grace and truth*'. Truth may be found in unexpected places of vulnerability. Grace is found in raw and broken places. Jesus is identified as light shining in the darkness, and he becomes part of raw, fleshly existence. The glory of God may be glimpsed in broken and uncertain places.

In the Prologue something new is occurring. The Incarnation is an act of grace and risk-taking. Jesus comes into the world to continue God's creative work. He comes to reveal God in acts of grace and truth in the midst of ordinary, messy life. The Prologue brings hope to our world. In times of uncertainty and confusion the creative purposes of God may be seen.

At Christmas Jesus once again comes as the Word made flesh. He comes as light into the dark places of our world. The light is shining in the darkness, and the darkness cannot put out the light.

Prayer:

This Christmas Day we worship you,
the Word made flesh,
born among us as one of us,
sharing our dreams and fears.

Open our eyes to see your glory
in unexpected places
and your grace and truth
in broken and tense places.
Your light bringing brightness to the world.

Susan Miller

26th December (Boxing Day)

Bible reading:

When they heard these things, they became enraged and ground their teeth at Stephen …

While they were stoning Stephen, he prayed, 'Lord Jesus, receive my spirit.' Then he knelt down and cried out in a loud voice, 'Lord, do not hold this sin against them.' When he had said this, he died.

Acts 7:54, 59–60

When I was given the scripture passage for today's reflection, I had to go back and read it again to make sure that I had the right passage for the day after Christmas. It didn't seem quite right to reflect on the stoning of Stephen right after leaving the peace and beauty of the manger. Of course, we are familiar with violence the week after Christmas when a threatened Herod kills all male children under the age of two.

But then I began to ponder this story from the Book of Acts about one of the first Christian martyrs. And the more I reflected, the more I realised that it is a perfect lens for the second day of Christmastide. I have always been somewhat awed by Stephen, the deacon who *'brimming with God's grace and energy, was doing wonderful things among the people, unmistakable signs that God was among them'* (Acts 6:8, *The Message*).[1]

God among us, or, as Eugene Peterson also says in his Bible translation *The Message*: 'The Word became flesh and blood, and moved into the neighborhood' (Jn 1:14).[2] Yesterday, on Christmas Day, we celebrated the Incarnation, our God, who in love, is willing to move into our neighborhoods. The enfleshed God, Jesus, who walks our streets, who stands beside those in intensive care units who are battling the Covid-19 virus, who accompanies us in our fear of the future and our exhaustion with the present. Jesus who allows us to see exactly what God's love looks like.

And Stephen was also able to incarnate this love in his life. Whenever I meet a Christian who is a powerful witness to me of Christ's love and grace, I always wonder who God used to shape them. Stephen, full of grace and power, must have been shaped by the Holy Spirit in community. He spoke the difficult truth in love to those who did not want to hear that truth. They spread fake news about him. But when they brought him before the council of religious leaders, they stared intently at him, and they saw that *'his face was like the face of an angel'* (Acts 6:15, NRSV). An angel, a messenger of God, stands before them speaking truth in love.

But when they hear God's truth from Stephen's mouth, they become enraged and grind their teeth at Stephen. There has been a lot of grinding of teeth this year in the face of the pandemic, and once again exposing the lack of justice for people of colour. We often don't like to hear the truth, even when it is shared in love. We too like our fake news, and we have so many more ways to share fake news than did those in the time of Stephen.

They cannot stand to hear God's truth, so they do what folks have continued to do ever since that time. They turn to violence. They cover their ears and with a loud shout all rush together against him. Like they did with Jesus, they drag Stephen out of the city, and begin to stone him.

But the part of this story which continues yesterday's Christmas story is the way Stephen responds to their violence. Filled with the Holy Spirit, he gazes into heaven, and like the shepherds, sees the glory of God and Jesus standing at the right hand of God. God's power in Stephen is not just in the great wonders and signs he did among the people, but in the wonder and sign of the way he dies.

While they are stoning him, he prays. He knows how Jesus dies, and he chooses in his death to incarnate Christ's love. *'Lord, do not hold this sin against them.'* He forgives. He loves. He has the face of an angel, a messenger of God.

With all the division in our troubled world today, this story is a lens of how we are also called to live and die. When surrounded by those who see things in such a different way or whom I perceive don't seem to care about the welfare of others, I am tempted to grind my teeth and respond with disdain. But Stephen challenges me to be a messenger of that love which was born at Bethlehem.

Prayer:

Thank you, Lord, for the risk you took when you entered our world in love. Help me to risk living in the way of your love. Amen

John McCall

Note:

1. & 2. Scripture quotations from THE MESSAGE, copyright © 1993, 2002, 2018 by Eugene H. Peterson. Used by permission of NavPress. All rights reserved. Represented by Tyndale House Publishers, Inc.

First Sunday after Christmas Day

Bible reading:

'Master, now you are dismissing your servant in peace,
    according to your word;
for mine eyes have seen your salvation,
    which you have prepared in the presence of all peoples,
a light for revelation to the Gentiles,
    and for glory to your people Israel.'

Luke 2:29–32 (NRSV)

Reflection:

About thirty years ago Jim Wallis, the American Evangelical social activist, visited Edinburgh. At a meeting in the University Chaplaincy, he gave a radical challenge to faith and political action, and ended with a word of encouragement. At that time the peace movement seemed to have faltered and become weary and disillusioned. The heady days when we thought that nuclear weapons, and even war, could soon be banished for ever, seemed now to be very distant. But Wallis reminded us that our faith demanded endurance for the long haul, and the end, although certain, would not necessarily be apparent to us. As the meeting finished, an elderly colleague in ministry, Douglas Crawford, turned to me. 'That's the message,' he said. 'We are not called to success, but to faithfulness.'

I have often thought of these words of Douglas when reading or hearing the prayer of Simeon that has become a standard part of the liturgy in many churches at this time of year, and is known as the Nunc Dimittis. This is often sung in the evening, almost as a restful and comforting word, but of course it is much more dynamic than that. We know very little about Simeon, and this encounter with Mary, Joseph and the baby Jesus is found only in Luke's Gospel. But in a few words we have a picture of a good and devout man who served God and looked forward in hope, not just to the One who comes for Israel, but for the salvation, the healing, of the world.

He believed that in his lifetime he would see a sign that would indicate the longed-for Messiah. And he had the insight to recognise it in the most unlikely place and in the most unlikely way.

It is probable that Simeon was then an elderly and a respected worshipper, if not leader, in the temple. It is impressive that even in the presence of a small and vulnerable baby brought by parents, whose poverty was indicated by the cheapest sacrificial offering of two doves, he was ready to let go of his responsibilities and be content that others would continue his faithful service. The 'letting go' without a completion of the dream is a great lesson to any who have given much in pursuit of their vision. People who take up the reins of other leaders in public life, great causes, charities, and perhaps especially in religious groups, often face a difficult task, if their predecessors fail to let go. 'Founder's Syndrome' is an all too familiar pattern.

I remember from schooldays a verse of a familiar hymn which ran: '*When comes the promised time that war shall be no more, and lust, oppression, crime, shall flee thy face before?*'[1] That question has countless echoes in our present world where oligarchs, demagogues and crooked systems on all continents display all of these vices, and where the poor and the vulnerable suffer from the resulting tyranny. Yet that world would also be familiar to Old Simeon. He knew well the human costs of a brutal occupation and the collusion of a religious elite, who kept their position through spiritual domination. But he reached into the heart of his faith and found hope.

We, in a post-Enlightenment Europe and America, have all too often confused hope with optimism that progress would continue. Simeon was too wise to buy that one. He warned Mary and Joseph, as he gave them his blessing, that this child was to be a sign that would be opposed, and that his honest unmasking of human behaviour would lead to a violent response. Perhaps he foresaw the need for them all to become refugees in Egypt from Herod's oppression, or even that this witness to truth would take Jesus to the Cross. '*A sword will pierce your own soul*' are the words that Luke reports.

In April 1968 in the speech known as 'I've been to the Mountaintop', delivered hours before he was killed, Dr Martin Luther King echoed old Simeon.

He admitted to difficult days ahead and to his wish to live a long life. But he said wasn't concerned about that. He just wanted to serve God, no longer fearing death. He gave thanks that, like Moses, he had been given a vision over the mountaintop to the place that he would in all probability never see. But he finished his speech with the words: *'I'm not worried about anything. I'm not fearing any man. Mine eyes have seen the glory of the coming of the Lord.'*

We in our time can feel linked to those who have gone before, when we say in the Iona liturgy that we *'affirm God's goodness at the heart of humanity, planted more deeply than all that is wrong'.*

Prayer:

When the parties are over,
when the friends and relations have gone home,
when the balloons are burst – the mince pies reduced to crumbs –
the cards and the paper in the recycle bin,
God says: 'Here I am, knocking on your door.'

When the fireworks have become damp squibs,
the 'first foots' gone home to their beds,
the swimmers in the River Forth thawed out,
the bottles smashed in the bottle bank,
God says: 'Here I am, knocking on your door.'

You say to us – your reluctant people:
'Let me in, and I will show you new ways.'
But we like the ways of all our last years –
our past years – before this coming one,
the comfort of familiarity, the safety of the tried and the known.

You say to us: 'I will lead you out of your comfort zone
to where dreams become reality.
Where dull routine can be transformed into challenge and adventure.
I will light your way into this New Year of possibilities.
For you – for those who follow.'

We are human – we are easily discouraged – the dark Covid days and
the cold have taken their toll.
The Christmas lights that shone in our darkness are extinguished.

Give us the courage to follow your light
along the road of compassion, of peace, of community,
so that we can become the people you created us to be.
God says: 'Here I am – knocking on your door.'
The door opens – the New Year is ahead – the adventure is beginning.

Iain and Isabel Whyte

Note:

1. 'Thy kingdom come, O God', by Lewis Hensley (1824–1905)

28th December

Bible reading:

Praise the Lord from the earth,
*   you sea monsters and all deeps,*
fire and hail, snow and frost,
*   stormy wind fulfilling his command!*

Psalm 148:7–8 (NRSV)

Reflection:

People really are afraid of what they do not know, aren't they? Have you ever met a sea monster? Me neither, but they sound pretty scary! I bet they sounded even more terrifying when the psalmist was writing. There weren't professional marine biologists back then ready to tell them that there is no such thing as a sea monster, and to explain, in detail, the biology of creatures under the sea! There are still creatures in the sea that we are afraid of, often with good reason.

We are still afraid, though, of what we do not know. As we continue to grapple with Covid-19 and it's ongoing ramifications, many of us are afraid. As we continue to expose and respond to the environmental crisis, many of us are afraid. As society continues to grow and change and experience and respond to poverty and oppression and pain ... many of us are afraid. We are afraid because we don't know what's going to happen to us and to future generations. We are afraid because we feel that we can't change enough, quick enough. We are afraid, if we are truly honest, because we wonder whether we might be part of the problem. Here be monsters, and perhaps, at times, we are the monsters.

This sea monster verse reminds me of the story about that time that Jesus was sound asleep while everyone else was panicking about a storm ... They seemed pretty annoyed by the time they managed to wake him up. They didn't get why he was so calm. But, ignoring their panic, he calmed the storm quickly, efficiently, powerfully, and asked, 'Why do you have so little faith?' I kind of feel sorry for them. They were really scared of something that was genuinely dangerous, and their leader is questioning their faith?

Did the Psalmist have more faith than Jesus' disciples? Somehow, I doubt it! Rather, I reckon most of us have just a tiny seed of faith. Some days we can picture that mustard plant shooting up from the fertile ground. On other days, it feels like we are struggling to rise up through the hard, cracked ground. That is a part of being human. It is enough. You are enough. Our fears, rational and irrational, arise out of memories and thoughts and feelings and experiences.

But, perhaps, we need to water our seeds, and not our fear. Where is your attention? Is it with your fear or with your hope? Which do you spend time cultivating each day? What resources might help you to grow hope?

One of the types of fear that I haven't mentioned is the fear that humans (intentionally or unintentionally) cause others. I wonder if you might make elevating kindness above fear part of your daily spiritual practice?

Meditation:

Breathe in … breathe out …
Breathe in … breathe out …
Breathe in peace … breathe out fear …
Breathe in mystery … breathe out fear …
Breathe in love … breathe out fear …
Breathe in hope … breathe out fear …
Breathe in kindness … breathe out fear …
Breathe in … breathe out …
Breathe in … breathe out …

Action:

Consider becoming part of the movement to make kindness the norm, by becoming a 'RAKtivist' (Random Acts of Kindness activist).
See https://www.randomactsofkindness.org

Alex Clare-Young

29th December

Bible reading:

While he was still speaking to the crowds, his mother and his brothers were standing outside, wanting to speak to him. Someone told him, 'Look, your mother and your brothers are standing outside, wanting to speak to you.' But to the one who had told him this, Jesus replied, 'Who is my mother, and who are my brothers?' And pointing to his disciples, he said, 'Here are my mother and my brothers! For whoever does the will of my Father in heaven is my brother and sister and mother.'

Matthew 12:46–50 (NRSV)

Reflection:

The young girl smiles timidly from beneath the heavenly blue cloak. The young boy looks mostly down at the floor, nervously adjusting the strange head covering that sometimes slips over his eyes. There is an array of shepherds, a few simply adorable sheep, maybe a cow or donkey. Angels for sure, grins as bright as their halos, so proud of their particular status. Wings sometimes get in the way of others; there is a little jostling. The kings will arrive later. No brothers or sisters around yet. The baby in the manger is the eldest child in his family.

It seems likely that this beloved vision of the holy family united in pageant form was not 'in person' this year. A regular family visiting six feet apart during Covid is one thing. Spreading out the members of this Christmas scene, though, does not work. It is the intimacy of family, animals and strangers and angels and kings, notwithstanding, that makes it work.

We know the birth narrative to be an imaginative story constructed by gospel writer Luke alone. But the passage for today relating to the adult family of Jesus appears in all three synoptic gospels, and in the Gospel of Thomas. Its appearance in the latter creates a greater degree of authenticity for me, as the Gospel of Thomas is an earlier, straightforward listing of the 'sayings' of Jesus, with fewer of the added contextual trappings of the early

church found in the later gospels. This dismissal of his family of origin –
'*who is my mother, and who are my brothers?*' – is actually one of relatively
few lines that folks agree the historical Jesus really did say.

So, I need to listen closely.

As a mother, I wince at the words ascribed to Jesus in this passage, as I do
when he gets a bit snarky with his mum about the wine at the wedding in
Cana. I get it. It is our job as parents to let go and rejoice when we feel our
children have established themselves securely and happily within their
calling. Right? But having said that, the scripture passage for today from
Matthew's Gospel deletes the tense context chronicled in the Gospel of
Mark: Jesus has returned home and is facing some neighbours who think
that he is possessed by Satan. The neighbours call his family to restrain
him. He dismisses the restraint, taking the opportunity to make his point
about family and community (Mk 3:31–35).

Chronicled by Matthew or not, chances are good there is serious tension
in the air for this scene. And we are witnesses. In just a few days, the lectionary would have us travel from the intimate family scene in the stable
to a situation that a family therapist might label as pretty dysfunctional.

That might be just the point. There is nothing normal about this man.
Indeed, most everything he does and the words he utters challenge the pre-
vailing norms. For one thing, he is over thirty and not married, even
though he seems to rather like the company of women. He seems set on
surrounding himself with an unconventional group of friends hanging on
to every word that comes out of his mouth. Yet he says it is not their def-
erence to him that makes them family. It is what they do, how they act.

I wonder: Is that how we might define family-outside-of-family? When we
say someone is 'like family' to us, we usually mean there is an intimacy to
our friendship similar to what we would have with parent or sibling.
Although all of us have instances of decrying the actions of family members
and friends who are 'like family', in the end, our love for them is not con-
ditioned on how they act.

I understand: the point of this statement by Jesus in this gospel passage is not really to dismiss his family of origin. Instead, it is an invitation to us to become close enough with Jesus that we can call him 'brother'. But that closeness is not automatic, he says, it is earned by how we act.

And maybe that is why the passage still makes me wince. Because this is the difference between Jesus and God for me. Nothing can separate us from the love of God. It is pure grace, not earned. Mary's heart is like that of God. This reprimand, while making an important, larger point about our actions in response to God, still pierces the heart of the mother of the babe in the manger.

Prayer:

Dear mothering God, help us to extend familial love unconditionally to those around us who provide us with the support we need to do the work that you have given us to do, that we might, in turn, support theirs.

Action:

Reach out today to a member of your family or a close friend who has been acting in a way that distresses you. And listen.

Katharine M Preston

30th December

Bible reading:

Praise the Lord!
Praise the Lord from the heavens;
  praise him in the heights!
Praise him, all his angels;
  praise him, all his hosts!

Praise him, sun and moon;
  praise him, all you shining stars!
Praise him, you highest heavens,
  and you waters above the heavens!

Psalm 148:1–4 (NRSV)

I am writing this in one of the hottest weeks I've ever known in the UK; I'm hiding in the shade and praying for the humidity to break. It is hard to get into the mindset of winter in weather like this, but this psalm speaks into every month and I hope my thoughts are as appropriate in the cold of late December as in the heat of August.

Psalm 148 is a wonderful psalm of praise to God, a poem of celebration of the world around us and a song of love for the planet God entrusted to us. Reading the psalm reminded me today not just of our own desire to praise God but of the ways in which the whole planet praises God, in ways so much more direct than we might realise.

Flowers turn to the sun, reaching for the life-giving rays in thankfulness and praise, offering up their nectar for insects as part of an interconnected world.

Trees are complex ecosystems, supporting life in all its abundance: feeding, sheltering, nurturing, sustaining.

Animals eat only what they need, leaving the rest for other animals or to bless the earth; wasting none of God's precious creation.

I wonder how we praise God by our very existence. Whether we give back in praise as much as we take from the planet.

We are blessed by the world and are given the responsibility by God to care for it; but do we see that as part of our Christian life? As part of praising God?

Psalm 148 inspired Saint Francis of Assisi to compose the 'Canticle of the Sun', praising God for all of creation. St Francis had a great love for animals and the environment and spent much of his time teaching that the world was created good and beautiful by God; and that we have a duty to care for it as praise to God. In the 21st century, eight hundred years after St Francis' ministry, we are called even more to care for creation, to fight climate injustice and to give praise to God through our protection of the environment. Speaking of St Francis, you might, in this Christmas season, remember, or be interested to discover, that he created the first live Nativity scene.

I have always found myself feeling the greatest connection to God in the natural world, amongst trees or along shorelines, watching reflections on lakes or listening to birdsong. It is in these places that I have felt the calming stillness of God, the blessing of his creation and the truth of my place in the world.

Four years ago a group of us started a Forest Church in a nature reserve in the middle of our suburban community: we wanted to provide a place for people to come together and worship God in the natural cathedral of woods and meadows. Over the months of lockdown in 2020 the blessings of these connections with nature have developed for us, and so many others, as daily walks became time for gratitude for wild places and tiny gardens became providers of vegetables and flowers. In the hardest of times it has been the God of creation who has been close to us and given us signs of light and celebration.

Action:

As you go through your day, take time to notice God in the world about you and praise Him. Find a plant or flower, a cloud or a drop of rain and spend just a few minutes marvelling at the wonder of creation.

Ask God to show you lessons you could learn from this part of the planet and to be with you as you continue to live as a guardian of the earth.

Then praise God for the fish of the sea and the birds of the sky; for the snow, mist and rain; for the sun through the clouds; for the mountains and hills, the valleys and plains; for the trees and the bushes; for the insects, animals and all of humankind.

Prayer:

Alleluia.
Praise the Lord.
Wherever you go
praise the Lord!

Praise the sun
rising each dawn.

Praise the moon
lighting the night.

Praise the wind
scattering seeds.

Praise the rain
sustaining all blessings.

Praise the earth and all of her creatures.
Praise the water as hope-filled conveyer.
Praise all of creation in life-giving action.
Care for the planet in each prayerful habit.

Alleluia.
Praise the Lord.
Wherever you go
praise the Lord!

Emma Major

31st December

Bible reading:

Again Jesus spoke to them, saying, 'I am the light of the world. Whoever follows me will never walk in darkness but will have the light of life.'

John 8:12 (NRSV)

Will Hogmanay be celebrated in Scotland tonight? Will folks everywhere join in singing 'Auld Lang Syne', or will we still be singing laments? Will there be fireworks over the Opera House in Sydney, a lightshow at the Arc de Triomphe, lanterns lit in South Korea? Will the ball drop in a jam-packed Times Square? Or will we still be sheltering, quarantining, shielding, cocooning in those places where we have spent most of this year.

In this year of uncertainty, of the pandemics of illness as well as anger, of so many things postponed, cancelled or simply forgotten, it is hard to say what this night might be like (or at least as I write this at the end of summer 2020, it is).

Yet, as it has always been, this is a day/evening in which to reflect, to look back on the past 12 months, to remember all that has happened, or not.

So many, including some of us, lost their jobs. So many kids, including some of ours, and some of us, lost school, sports, plays, music, and more importantly, those friendships which mean so much to our development as human beings. So many went without that human touch of a hand, a hug, a kiss, which seems so simple, yet reminds us of our value to others, and the meaning of their lives to us. We lost that taken-for-granted community called church, which we now know is far more of a family than an institution for most of us. And far too many of us lost a parent, a grandparent, another family member, a partner, a friend, a neighbour, a co-worker to this terrible virus.

We sat in the self-imposed isolation of our homes and flats; we walked in the dawn or as dusk fell, in the hope we would not encounter another person; we sewed masks for others, and struggled to learn how to wear them to protect others from ourselves. We found ourselves worn down by the boredom of being bored, and grew weary from the disruption of those everyday joys that we never noticed filled us with joy – sharing a brief conversation with the same clerk at the shop, going into a bookstore or library simply to walk down the aisles of books, sharing a pint with a friend at the pub. As bright as the sun grew as the months grew longer, it seemed that we still found ourselves in the shadows of life.

But it is precisely in the shadows that we are most likely to encounter the Light of Christ. And we did, didn't we, these last months in this endless year? …

The light that broke out in the lonely neighbourhoods as children and youth pulled chairs out onto porches, balconies, sidewalks so that they could offer impromptu concerts for the folks who lived around them.

That light we discovered in that crotchety old neighbour who has never had a kind word to say about anyone, but who called people on the street each and every day to simply say, 'So how are you doing? Is there anything I can do for you today?'

The light that we saw at the end of the tunnel in the folks in hospitals and research centres who work night and day to try to find a vaccine to fight the virus. As well as the light in the souls of the volunteers who are willing to be injected in trial programmes.

The light that has always shined in the gentleness, the goodness, the love and the hope in all those around us.

Suggestion:

However you celebrate or observe this day, take a moment to think about:

– where the light appeared in your life this year (because it did);

– who was the light for you (for there was at least one person);

– and how you were the light someone else needed (because you were).

Thom M Shuman

New Year's Day

Bible reading:

He has made everything suitable for its time; moreover he has put a sense of past and future into their minds, yet they cannot find out what God has done from the beginning to the end. I know that there is nothing better for them than to be happy and enjoy themselves as long as they live; moreover, it is God's gift that all should eat and drink and take pleasure in all their toil.

Ecclesiastes 3:11–13 (NRSV)

Making the conscious choice to trust in God and to believe that he still cares for us is one of the hardest things to do. Forgetting God's presence in everyday life gives you the opening to worry constantly. When we get into the habit of expecting the worst it can be a comfort: we will either be prepared for the worst, or be pleasantly surprised when things don't go too badly. Forgetting or not trusting in God's benevolence is easy, but it strips the joy from day-to-day life.

At the time of writing this, I am still furloughed, due to the coronavirus lockdown, from my work in the hospitality industry. I live in fear of being let go without warning. When my boss phoned me last week, my thoughts immediately turned to the chasm that would open up beneath me if I was to be let go. When I answered I spoke from a place of fear. And so I missed out on her pleasant and unthreatening conversation. She was simply checking on how I was and letting me know how the café was coping.

Until the call ended I couldn't relax, something I only realised after we'd said our goodbyes. I missed out on having a genuinely thoughtful catch-up with a wonderful woman. I think living with this sense of trepidation from moment to moment is not so unusual for many. It's easier for us to choose fear over trust. If I had simply trusted that God knew what was going to happen, and that he would make sure that, no matter what, I would remain safe with him, I might have been able to accept the phone call for what it was rather than what I feared it may have been. Choosing to trust in God rather than reside in human fear is, I believe, what God wishes us all to do.

The way I see it, Ecclesiastes 3:11–13 is essentially asking us to trust that even if we can't comprehend the bigger picture, trusting in God's love is the best thing we can possibly do. Naturally, it's easier said than done, especially as there doesn't seem to be a step-by-step list of instructions on how to let the fear of the unknown slide into the belief that truly God has made everything suitable for its time, and therefore knows what the bigger picture looks like regardless of how blind we are. Still, I think the first step is realisation. I know that I don't want to spend next year in unnecessary fear over what I either don't know or can't change.

So, this coming year, when coronavirus still poses a significant threat for many, I will practise accepting things as they are, and trust in God's complete benevolence.

Trusting in God can seem terrifying – it's a real leap of faith – but a conscious trust in God is brave and so very rewarding. We may not ever find out what God has done from the beginning to the end for us, but we can believe that God's kindness has no limits, and whatever he has done from the beginning to end is good. I think that if I can accept God's ineffable plan for me, I'll be able to live in a little more joy. I'm going to try to trust that God is good, even though I can't see the bigger picture.

Action:

This recipe for banana bread is cheap, simple and delicious. Make it (or another recipe you like) and share it. Let all eat and drink and take pleasure. 2021, and any new year, may seem scary, but we can trust in God's love, and know that we can still eat and take pleasure together:

Ingredients:

100g margarine
225g caster sugar
1 egg

3 large ripe bananas
225g self-raising flour
1 teaspoon baking soda
1 teaspoon vanilla essence
50g walnuts, chopped (optional)

Oven at 180°C, 350°F, Gas mark 4

Method:

Grease and line a medium-sized loaf tin.
Beat the margarine and sugar.
Add the beaten egg and mashed bananas and mix well.
Add the flour and baking soda and mix well.
Add the vanilla essence and walnuts.
Pour mix into loaf tin and bake for roughly 60 minutes.[1]

Laura Gisbourne

Notes:

1. From *More than a Meal: A Cookbook in Support of the Homeless* © St George's
   Church & Crypt, Leeds, 1998. Used with permission.

   'St George's Church & Crypt is a charity working with the homeless, the vulnerable and those suffering from addiction' (www.stgeorgescrypt.org.uk).

2nd January

Bible reading:

Who is wise and understanding among you? Show by your good life that your works are done with gentleness born of wisdom.

James 3:13 (NRSV)

Reflection:

Living on the edge of a continent, and with a sense of being on the edge of history, too, the small resident group on Iona has been living a form of community life echoing medieval monasticism as well as the summer camps of work and worship led by George MacLeod. There have been fewer visitors to the island in 2020, because of Covid and lockdown, and a greater opportunity to pay attention to our common life.

From the daily rhythm of our morning worship, our work, our eating together and our shared accommodation, a way of living has emerged that none of us will forget.

Is this the good life? Are our works done with gentleness born of wisdom? Are we wise and understanding?

The stories of Columba and his monks, the Benedictines in the Abbey and the Augustinian nuns have been of more immediate interest to us than simply a backdrop to twenty-first century community life on Iona. To live well with each other, we discovered painfully, it was necessary not only to spend time together, but to have privacy to reflect and just be. The architecture of the Abbey began to make more sense to us: compact cells or bedrooms for individual use and large communal rooms (Chapter House, Refectory, Abbey Church) for gathering together.

The Daily Office of the Iona Community comes from this monastic tradition; it is prescriptive and has very little flexibility for adding personal prayers or flourishes. As the days and months have gone by, this rigidity, which once seemed to straitjacket our worship, has turned out to be its strength. Whatever happens amongst us as a community or in world events, the Daily Office remains. It rolls on regardless, providing a steady heartbeat during uncertain times.

A separate pattern has been a time of silence together each week. The Iona Community's prayers include this: 'Nearer are you than breathing, closer than hands and feet. Ours are the eyes with which you, in the mystery, look out with compassion on the world.'[1] An extended time in stillness with God, hearing the steady breathing in and out of the people next to you, is an intimate experience. It's hard not to care about someone whose fragile humanity has been so close.

Each day our morning worship contains these lines: 'we confess to turning away from God in the way we wound our lives, the lives of others, and the life of the world'.[2] Saying these words together, day by day, when the hurts and angers of living together are still raw, can be bewildering and shocking. It can also propel us to address the dissonance and, more often than not, to reveal the conflicts within ourselves.

Dietrich Bonhoeffer warned of being in love with the idea of community, rather than the warts-and-all community that we are actually part of. He must have been frustrated with the lack of gentleness, wisdom and understanding in his seminary. Yet he may have been surprised by a deep joy to find depths of understanding and unexpected wisdom over the washing-up, or through a small act of kindness or bravery.

Seen through the lens of our experience of the common life, the intractable conflicts on the world stage cry out for a softening, a bending to each other. Living in community takes time. Understanding and wisdom need space and commitment to flourish. We can't simply switch each other off. We meet again at the next meal, and the next, and the next. When transformation occurs, when the connection is made, when gentle wisdom emerges, it brings tears of recognition to adult eyes.

The Daily Office has sustained our life together on the edge of the Atlantic, linking us through history to earlier communities. It also links us through geography to the wider Iona Community, whose members each say the same prayers as we do, day by day, in its work for justice and peace.

Columba once asked one of his monks to go down to the shore and meet a wounded visitor. 'Bring him back and look after him,' he said, 'until he is well enough to continue on his way.' The visitor turned out to be a heron with a broken wing. In time, the heron flew off on its way. Near the Abbey we have occasionally seen a handsome heron in low, majestic flight and it reminds us of this story of gentle hospitality.

Prayer:

Wise and gentle God, infuse us with enough patience and curiosity
to understand the strange and the hostile,
so that divisions can be healed, justice realised
and all may have life in its fullness.

Catriona Robertson

Notes:

1. From a prayer by George MacLeod, *Iona Abbey Worship Book*, Wild Goose Publications, 2017

2. From *Iona Abbey Worship Book*, Wild Goose Publications, 2017

3rd January

Bible reading:

The storyteller, the uninvited, unrecognised one, came and lived with us.

John 1:14 (from my remembered Bible)

As I took the paddle for the first mile, I saw the beach getting smaller. The sound of the pebbles rattling on the shore receded and was replaced in my head by the sound of bullets and explosions. A bird cried out – I thought it was my sister screaming.

By the second mile, the land had nearly gone. How I remembered that land, softly, gently rising and falling. Where had the trees gone? We crested the swell and the sea went on and on and on.

By the third mile, we were entirely surrounded by water. There was silence in the boat and we were barely breathing so as not to rock it about or displace the person next to us. A woman fumbled with her shawl, trying desperately to put her baby to her breast as carefully as possible, and we reached out to steady her.

By the fourth mile, I thought: *we will not make it.* Anxiety was rising up in every chest, threatening to spew out those last few pieces of bread we had snatched on the shore. There was nothing to drink. Sea water spilled into the boat.

By the fifth mile, there were more birds following us, mocking and wheeling overhead. They were like the crowds at the gates of the camp: 'Go home, go home, go home,' they called, their words streaming out behind us.

By the sixth mile, I willed my hands to hold the paddle, my arms to dip it in the water, my shoulders and back to push it through the water. A jelly-fish appeared and I envied it. Feeling just like jelly myself, how I wished I could slip into the water and become part of it.

By the seventh mile, there were huge ships on the horizon in every direction, yet they seemed oblivious to us. We were like the tiniest insect on the surface of the sea.

By the eighth mile, I tried to remember my parents and all they'd told me about hope and love, how they'd shown me, every day, how one person should treat another. I repeated their names under my breath, hoping that I'd get the opportunity to repeat them to my own children one day.

By the ninth mile, the hope in my heart kept being swallowed up by anger and I thought of those who had pushed us into the sea and taken our money. The phone they'd given us did not even work.

By the tenth mile, I saw a fleet of clouds sailing above the white cliffs of the far shore. That was the land, the place I'd heard of, and my tears joined the salty water in the bottom of the boat.

By the eleventh mile, I knew we were losing the fight. The cliffs did not get closer, the boat was letting in more water and we were all getting weaker. A small child peered out from under her mother's arm. I dipped my paddle again.

By the twelfth mile, it felt like a thousand or more. It felt like every mile we'd already come was strung one on another, like pearls on a rotten string.

By the thirteenth mile, I was ready to give up, as was everyone else in the boat.

By the fourteenth mile, I was sure we were no longer moving.

By the fifteenth mile, I watched as someone tried the phone again. Rage burst up inside me and I cried out, 'Why are we forsaken?' and those around me wept or turned away.

By the sixteenth mile, a small boat seemed to shadow us, stealthily at first. It was difficult to attract its attention without rocking the boat. A woman held up a red scarf and it flew out behind us, declaring our presence to the whole world.

By the seventeenth mile, the boat had got nearer and I saw people were photographing us. In the boat, questions were asked. 'What are they doing?' 'Why do they not help us?' I didn't know then that they were preparing breakfast for the people on the white cliffs, who like to see us suffering while eating their morning meal.

By the eighteenth mile, they finally seemed to understand, and told us they had phoned for help. We sighed with relief and many prayers were murmured.

By the nineteenth mile, I could see a small boat speeding out to us, the throb of its engine and the calling of the crew cutting through the dead air. How far away was it now? The boat came alongside and we tried not to panic, handing up our precious cargo of young and old.

As I laid down my paddle, I could see the shore. God, have mercy ...

Reflection:

Did you know?

There's a place in Kent where all the old boats from the migrant crossings are kept, piled up one on another: the inflatables graveyard.

Take action:

If there is a local organisation helping refugees, support them today.

If the place where you live is a City of Sanctuary, https://cityofsanctuary.org, see if you can join in. If it is not, how could your community become such a place?

Prayer:

May we be the Sanctuary.

Janet Lees

4th January

Bible reading:

Come now, you who say, 'Today or tomorrow we will go to such and such a town and spend a year there, doing business and making money.' Yet you do not even know what tomorrow will bring. What is your life? For you are a mist that appears for a little while and then vanishes. Instead you ought to say, 'If the Lord wishes, we will live and do this or that.'

James 4:13–15 (NRSV)

James 4:13–15 conjures up fond memories of my late grandparents, affectionately known as Mamaw and Papaw. Papaw was the guardian of my childhood fishing exploits, which were generally divided into two categories: 1) the well-stocked catfish pond behind their farmhouse where we caught fish as fast as we could reel them in and 2) all other ponds and rivers in the area where we never caught anything but sunburns and mosquito bites.

Despite the guaranteed success of the catfish pond, which we could almost see from the kitchen window, Papaw was constantly plotting off-property fishing adventures for his blond-haired, short-sighted grandson. 'We'll take the johnboat to the slough of the White River.' 'We'll float the Strawberry.' 'There's a fishin' hole below the dam … We'll get up early and go on Thursday.' These were grandfather-grandson conversations that left Mamaw out of sight and out of mind – or, so we thought. But there she was: always within eavesdrop, always ready to pounce upon our plans: 'Dewell,' she'd say, calling Papaw by his first name, 'you don't go sayin' what you're gonna do on Thursday. You might be dead by then.' We'd look askance, but Mamaw always held sway. While growing memories together on his farm, Papaw and I spent the summer imagining fishing trips that got away.

It was sometime later – when I made my first forays into the New Testament – that I understood the magic words for making plans in Mamaw's house: *'If the Lord wishes, we will live and do this or that'* (v.15). Mamaw was a herald of James: *'You never know what tomorrow will bring'* (v.14). As a life-time member of Pilgrims Rest Baptist Church, Mamaw's Christian credentials were well-deserved. Sunday after Sunday, she'd wake up, still alive, and head down to the church, where she played the piano for over sixty years. Diverging at the crossroads, Papaw attended Campground Methodist Church.

Being with Papaw meant more to me than fishing, and Mamaw's castigations never did us any harm. Yet, approaches such as Mamaw's restrain the adventurous, limit life's abundance, and dampen the fullness of lived experience. James makes a vital point: all life – each and every day– is dependent upon God. But we need to move beyond the full stop. James goes on to tell us that we are but *'a mist that appears for a little while and then vanishes'* (v. 15). Far from telling us to do nothing, James is reminding us that we don't have long to act; he is urging us to live and to love. Mist lingers in the morning before dissipating in the daylight. Make hay while the sun is shining. Night comes before we know it.

While Mamaw liked asserting that life is contingent upon God, the profundity of James is captured in the directness of the four-word question: *'What is your life?'* A gift of God. A sacred trust. A brief journey between cradle and grave. Between the quips and quotes of my grandparents, life was celebrated. God was present in the mist which now lingers as memory. A 10-year-old boy gazes upon the face of his grandfather seeking not answers to questions but the companionship of one he holds dear. I do not know what tomorrow will bring, but I'm grateful for the yesterdays of lived experience.

A quarter century after their deaths, I'm living in Italy with my wife, Janet – far away from the Ozark farm, no longer in family hands. In two days, the Epiphany procession of the Magi, one of my favorite Italian traditions, will pass through the streets of Milan, and – if God is willing and the creek don't rise – I'll see the sacred pageantry once again. In some ways, we never leave home. Or, the gospel story comes to us, embodied in those around us. I realise now that Mamaw was a Magi and Papaw was a wiseman, who, throughout their lives, gave precious gifts to grandsons and Christ childs alike. The Magi went home by another way, and we, too, following those before us, must journey – who knows when? – to the *'undiscovered country from whose bourn no traveller returns'*.

What is your life?

Words of reflection:

Thus says the Lord:
Stand at the crossroads, and look,
   and ask for the ancient paths,
where the good way lies; and walk in it,
   and find rest for your souls.

Jeremiah 6:16 (NRSV)

Rodney Aist

5th January

Bible reading:

Do to others as you would have them do to you.

Luke 6:31 (NRSV)

'Do to others as you would have them do to you' is sometimes known as 'The Golden Rule'. It is a phrase I was familiar with long before I knew where to find it in the Bible. I must have been encouraged as a child to think about my behaviour towards others in these positive terms because I simply cannot remember a time when I did not know it. How would I wish to be treated? Treat others like that. It is a mantra everyone can live by. If you were to remove it from its immediate context, you don't need faith or a relationship with Jesus to be moved to live in this way.

However, this verse does not sit on its own. It effectively summarises the verses that come before it. We are to love our enemy, do good to those who hate us, bless those who curse us, and pray for those who abuse us. If one cheek is struck, we are to offer the other; if our coat is taken, we must offer our shirt as well. We are to give to all those who beg from us and, if something is taken from us, we are not to ask for it back. We are to do to others as we would have them do to us.

Jesus was not speaking to us about our friends and families. He took it for granted that we would treat well those we already love. Everyone does that, he said.

Rather, he was speaking of our enemies and those who do or wish us harm; those who would take something from us and be unwilling to give in return. Jesus would have us treat them as we would have them treat us. So, I ask myself, would I want my enemy to love me or my abuser to pray for me or the person from whom I have already taken their coat to give me their shirt as well?

Left to myself, I think probably not. I would be fairly satisfied if my enemy tolerated me and left me alone. Similarly, I would probably be content if those who would hurt me ceased to cause me pain and did me no harm. I am not sure I would require anyone to love me or bless me or give me their shirt when I had taken their coat. I think how I would wish to be treated would not be that demanding. It would be enough to be at peace with those who I might otherwise fear.

However, Jesus did not leave his throne in heaven for the footstool of earth so we could just rub along with one another. He came because, like enemies, we are the ones who are capable of hating, cursing and abusing; of striking, not sharing and taking. He came to restore us not just from enmity to friendship with God but to kinship. As believers in Jesus as the Son of God, we are beloved children of God. We are showered with the riches and blessings of our relationship with God.

If I would be satisfied with my enemy tolerating me, the Holy Spirit would not be. The love of Jesus for his world is a radical love of action and self-giving for the other. Do to others as you would have them do to you sits for each one of us in the wake of the cross. Jesus died for us while we were still sinners and he gave us his Holy Spirit to help us to do to others not just as we would have them do to us but to do to others as Jesus has already done for us.

Prayer:

Heavenly Father, holy and everlasting God,
you show kindness and mercy to the ungrateful and the wicked.
You show kindness and mercy to me.

Jesus, Prince of Peace and Saviour God,
you died for your enemies.
You died for me.

Holy Spirit, living presence of God,
fill me with your grace to love as God has loved me,
to give of myself as Jesus gave all for me,
to do as you do for me.
Amen

Sarah Dickinson

Epiphany

Bible reading:

When they had heard the king, they set out; and there, ahead of them, went the star that they had seen at its rising, until it stopped over the place where the child was. When they saw that the star had stopped, they were overwhelmed with joy. On entering the house, they saw the child with Mary his mother; and they knelt down and paid him homage. Then, opening their treasure chests, they offered him gifts of gold, frankincense, and myrrh. And having been warned in a dream not to return to Herod, they left for their own country by another road.

Matthew 2:9–12 (NRSV)

Reflection: Epiphany – Otherwise

Reading the story of the magi, the wise men, the astrologers, in the middle of a pandemic, I found some of it strangely familiar. During the last year, as well as needing to take responsibility for our own actions, and hoping that our political leaders will do the same, we have all relied on the work of experts and their judgement. Doctors, research scientists, epidemiologists: we've needed to listen to their advice. Government ministers have told us again and again that they have been 'guided by the science'. Maybe Herod would say he was doing the same:

Then Herod secretly called for the wise men and learned from them the exact time when the star had appeared. Then he sent them to Bethlehem, saying, 'Go and search diligently for the child; and when you have found him, bring me word so that I may also go and pay him homage.' (Mt 2:7–8, NRSV)

He wanted to draw on their experience, but he lied about his reasons. He saw this child, to whose birth the star was a sign, as a rival to his own power. He didn't want to pay homage but to put paid to this threat. 'Guided by the science' – but with his own agenda.

The wise men of course were no fools (the clue is in the name). But they were at a disadvantage. For all their knowledge, their beliefs and values and the sense that this life-journey had meaning, they were now in an alien country, where they may not have understood the structures of power. Their experience, their integrity, may not have equipped them for this, just as the life-wisdom of ordinary people like ourselves may not protect us from coping with crisis, or being put down, patronised and manipulated by those who are supposed to be in charge.

The story tells of an encounter with Herod, an insecure ruler with shabby motives, in his palace in Jerusalem. But when they arrive in Bethlehem, and enter a simple village home or outhouse, all that foreboding turns to pure joy. The encounter with this child is an epiphany, a glimpse of God's glory. In a few words the Gospel paints a picture which we have seen again and again, in mosaics and frescoes and oil paintings and carvings and Christmas cards and Nativity plays: the richly dressed kings, kneeling in homage, the mother and child, symbolic gifts spilling from ornate caskets. We can dwell on this, as an image of deep devotion, and liturgical worship.

But for me the more challenging message is what comes next. The kings/wise men/magi don't stay long in this safe and sacred place. Nor do they conform to the expectations of Herod – that they'll go back the way they came, compliant with his plans.

That phrase about 'going back by another road … taking another way' makes me think about these words in a blog by Nick Baines, Bishop of Leeds:

'*Christian faith does not assume a life (or world) of continuous security and familiarity. It is fed by scriptures that speak of transience, mortality, provisionality, interruption and leavings. But, they also whisper that the endings are always beginnings – the leavings open a door to arrivals that could not have been experienced otherwise. In other words, the loss can be seen as a gift – what Walter Brueggemann calls "newness after loss".*'[1]

He posed four questions, which Iona Community Family Groups have been discussing:

1. *What have I/we lost that we need to regain in the weeks and months ahead?*

2. *What have we lost that needs to remain lost – left behind in another country?*

3. *What have I/we gained that we need to retain in the future?*

4. *What have we gained recently that was useful for this season but needs to be lost if we are to move forward?*[2]

Here's another way of reflecting on this Bible story and what Epiphany means in our present situation: a poem I wrote during lockdown.

Otherwise

They were wise, yes, they were well on in years.
Rich in experience, they left little to chance,
making careful calculations, taking responsibility.
They were well-travelled. They knew the world: it was theirs.
There were stars to guide them.
They could read the signs of the times.
It had taken a lifetime to come to this place:
they didn't always travel light;
they took many things for granted,
and others with a pinch of salt.
Salt-roads, silk-roads, the road less travelled,
open roads, opening up the world for them.
They were border-crossers, free to roam.
But where are they now, these wise men and women?

Patronised, put on the spot, put in their place by people in power,
sheltered, shielding, needing to admit vulnerability,
asking for directions, expected to do what they're told,
Underrated, frustrated. Lied to. Confused.
What price wisdom now?
Put on the spot, they give an honest answer.
Maybe they'll be co-opted, given a place in the plot.
Maybe not.
They listen and reflect. They can't give up on the star:
given half a chance, they'll get there. And they do.
They are astonished.

In a mean place, hopelessly confined,
an abundance of meaning they had forgotten,
a child who remembers, for them, who they once were:
an uncompromising embodiment of hope.
Here and now they can hand over the gifts
they have brought all this way – hand over much more.
Now they do not need to be in control.
It's not their guiding star any more;
it doesn't belong to the politicians
but to the children – vulnerable, visionary –
with a different way of seeing,
a different way of being.
And as they pause to wonder, lost for words,
the weight of carrying the world falls away.
Otherwise.

Knowing their emptiness, learning lightness of being,
they sleep.
Follow the logic of dreams, wake to another day.
Was it all a dream?
Was there an angel, they wonder, what did the angel say?

Everything has changed.
Take nothing for granted,
take a huge risk, take courage.
Go home by another way.

Jan Sutch Pickard

Note:

1. & 2. From 'Deep wells?', May 13, 2020, Musings of a Restless Bishop,
    https://nickbaines.wordpress.com

Appendix

Thursday in the fourth Week of Advent (when Christmas Eve falls on a Saturday)

Bible reading:

The word is near you,
  on your lips and in your heart.

Romans 10:8a (NRSV)

Reflection:

Christmas.
It's nearly here.

What's going on around you?
Are people cooking?
Are the shops bustling?
Is there snow?

What are the images around you?
Are the robins jolly?
Is Mary on a donkey?
Are there camels and kings?

Are there people around you?
Maybe friends and family?
Who is missing at your table?
Are you dining alone?

What's going on inside you?
Are you happy?
Are you sad?
Are you wondering and dreaming?

What's on the news today?
Where are people rejoicing?

Where are people hurting?
Who needs your money, your concern, your prayers?

Which words work for you today?
Rejoice? Be glad? Get ready?
Wow! I'm tired? I need you, Jesus?
Thank you? I'm struggling? No words, just sighs?

Christmas.
It's nearly here.
What still needs doing?

Look after yourself.
Look out for those who need love.

Reflective prayer:

The Word is near you,
on your lips
and in your heart.

You're that near, Jesus?
That close?

In my thinking,
in my speaking,
in my loving,
in my hopes and dreams?

Sometimes when I stop and feel and listen
I'm aware of your loving,
of being hugged,
of being blessed.

But mostly
I'm too busy to notice,
too busy writing and reading
and doing stuff that needs to be done.

Be near me today, Jesus,
be near me as you tell your story in me
and through me.

Help me to listen to my heart.

Action:

Read some of your Christmas cards.

Are there friends you want to contact?

Read or look at the news.

Do you want to share your resources? Pray? Be better informed?

Read or listen to a favourite Christmas story or poem or sing a Christmas song.

What are the words that grab you, challenge you, bless you, and why?

Chalk a Christmas message on your path or doorstep, or ask a child to do it for you.

Ruth Burgess

Friday in the fourth week of Advent (when Christmas Eve falls on a Saturday)

Bible readings:

Besides this, you know what time it is, how it is now the moment for you to wake from sleep.

Romans 13:11 (NRSV)

Sing to God a new song …

Psalm 96:1

Reflection:

Wake up.
The night is nearly over.
The stars are fading.
The earth is turning.
The day is almost here.

Wake up.
Wake up to who you are,
you belong to God.
You are loved and called to be loving.
You are called to love your neighbour as yourself.

Wake up.
Get moving!
It's time to leave the darkness behind you.
Get out of there,
you don't belong there any more.

Wake up.
Wake up to justice.
You are called to peacemaking.

You are called to be sober.
You are called to do good.

Wake up.
Wake up to what is happening.
Wake up to what God is doing.
Wake up now
to God moving in our midst.

Wake up.
The day is dawning.
Christmas is coming.

Open your eyes, stretch,
wriggle your toes and fingers.
Now is the moment to wake up to wonder.
You are called to walk in the light.

Psalm 96 (An all-age version)

Sing God a new song.
Sing all the earth.
Tell everyone of God's glory and justice.

Tell how God created the heavens.
Tell how God created the earth.
Tell of God's strength and God's beauty.

Be full of joy, sky.
Twinkle, stars.
Dance, planets.

Be glad, earth.
Wriggle, worms.
Grow, forests.

Roar out, loud sea.
Sing, whales.
Dive, gannets.

God is coming to earth.
God is coming with truth and integrity.
God is coming among us.

Sing God a new song.
Sing all the earth.
Tell everyone of God's glory and justice.

Prayer:

God of the morning,
wake me up.

Wake me up to rain and sunshine.
Wake me up to beauty.

Wake me up to hope and justice.
Wake me up to loving.

Wake me up to curiosity and wonder.
Wake me up to adventure.

God of the morning,
wake me up.

Wake me up good.

Action:

Try to make time to go for a slow walk today.

Enjoy shop windows. Walk among trees.

Put out a Christmas treat for the birds.

The Society of Friends talks of holding people and situations *in the light*.
Who and what do you want to hold in the light today?

Ruth Burgess

27th December
(in the years when this does not fall on a Sunday)

Bible readings:

… you shall see my back; but my face shall not be seen.

Exodus 33:23 (NRSV)

… God is light …

1 John 1:5 (NRSV)

Reflection:

'Maggie, you've got your teeth!'

Maggie stands in the fluorescent light of the homeless shelter and smiles, modeling them for us. 'Madonna, eat your heart out,' she says, and laughs in her husky, earthy way.

It's quite a contrast: the false perfection of the new, white-white teeth against the brown, wrinkled background of her crooked, beaten face.

It only took a year. 'Wait for your cheque.' 'Wait for your teeth.'

Maggie has learned patience. (Like everybody here, she's had to.) She knows it takes a long, long time for anything to trickle down to a night shelter in a basement. Having no teeth is a trial, but after so many trials and losses – abusive men, dead-end jobs, poor housing, psychiatrists and social workers, breast cancer; a best friend who lost all hope; a good friend who was murdered – you learn to endure, and to live with little things like having no teeth.

'You really look great, Mags,' I say.

'Well, thank you, dear, but they're just a plug in a leak, you know. The body dies, the soul is eternal, as they say. But at least I can chew now – no more soup and mush,' she says, and smiles brightly again.

'Alleluia,' I answer, and stop and gaze at her … But it's not her new white-white teeth I'm struck by – although I'm very happy she finally has them – it's her old laughing eyes – and the light that has never left her. The beautiful, strong light that no one has been able to blacken, or rob, take away, or put out. The miraculous, amazing light she has, somehow, never lost faith in.

Meditation:

In whose face have you glimpsed the face of God?

Neil Paynter

3rd January
(in the years when this does not fall on a Sunday)

Bible reading: Proverbs 1:20,29–31

Wisdom cries out in the street;
  in the squares she raises her voice …

Because they hated knowledge
  and did not choose the fear of the Lord,
would have none of my counsel,
  and despised all my reproof,
therefore they shall eat the fruit of their way
  and be sated with their own devices.

Reflection: A ninety-three-year-old woman talking about apples

'In ancient times we used to get all types of apples. We used to get Thamey Sweets, St Lawrence, crabs, russets, candy-striped, sheep's nose. Like a sheep's nose, yes. Sort of tapered. My mother would bake Thamey Sweets – and the skin would shine. So sweet you didn't need sugar. You just left the stem on and added cloves. A squatty kind of apple. God – the smell when they're baking,' sighed the old woman, and closed her eyes. Like it suddenly all came back to her. On a wave …

Prayer:

Thank you, God,
for the wisdom of ninety-three-year-old women:
food for thought.

Thank you for apples. For Thamey Sweet apples,
St Lawrence apples, crab apples,
russet apples, candy-striped apples,
sheep's nose apples ...

For the precious and amazing
diversity of your world.

May we never take that wealth for granted.
May we work to guard and secure it.
May we be full of wonder.

This we pray,
in the name of the One God:
the One God of many apples.
Amen

Thought:

Meditate on the fruit of God's Way ... Think about how you want to live
this year ...

Action:

Food Ethics Council: www.foodethicscouncil.org

Age UK: www.ageuk.org.uk

Neil Paynter

Sources and acknowledgements

About the contributors

Rodney Aist is a Methodist minister, pilgrimage author, and Holy Land scholar based in Milan, Italy. He directs a DMin in pilgrimage and spirituality through Drew Theological School in New Jersey. He is an associate of the Iona Community.

Ruth Burgess is a member of the Iona Community who lives in Dunblane. She is wondering what Advent and Christmas will be like this year, but she hopes to keep on walking by the river, writing and receiving Christmas greetings from family and friends, and enjoying the antics of the rooks and crows in her garden.

Revd Alex Clare-Young is a member of the Iona Community and Moderator of the LGBTQ+ Common Concern Network. Alex is a URC minister and ministers to a cyber church called Churspacious. Alex's first book, *Transgender. Christian. Human*, was published by Wild Goose in 2019.

Nancy Cocks, now retired from parish ministry, volunteers in refugee resettlement and continues writing in her hometown of Medicine Hat, Alberta, Canada. She is a former MacLeod Centre Warden.

Sarah Dickinson is an elder in the Church of Scotland and author of *While Swans Fly and Herons Wait* (Bramdean Press). Between 2004 and 2019, Sarah led contemplative prayer groups and retreats, for which she regularly wrote reflections.

Liz Dowler is a member of the Iona Community and of the Food Ethics Council, working with others for food justice and against health inequalities. She believes in sustainable food systems to change the world.

Laura Gisbourne, a founding member of the Iona Community Young Adults Group, works as a baker in an independent café in the North West of England. She gathers inspiration from her stunning local surroundings and personal experiences in life.

Urzula Glienecke, PhD, a Latvian theologian and activist finding her new church home in Scotland. Passionate about social justice, the environment and empowering people at the grassroots. A member of the Iona Community.

Tim Gorringe taught theology in India, Oxford, St Andrews and Exeter. For the past twelve years he has run a smallholding in Devon with his wife, Gill. His most recent book is *The World Made Otherwise* (Cascade, 2018), and a theology book, *Word and Silence,* is due out in the next few months (Fortress). He is a member of the Iona Community.

Ruth Harvey is the Leader of the Iona Community. Previously she was the Director of Place for Hope. She lives in Cumbria and is a member of the Society of Friends (Quakers) and a Church of Scotland minister.

Alison Jackson is a second year New Member of the Iona Community, Chair of Trustees of Church Action on Poverty until November 2020 and moderator of the CCN on Poverty and Inequality. She is a retired senior civil servant and lives in a small town just north of Bristol.

Janet Lees is a member of the Lay Community of St Benedict. She is the author of *Word of Mouth: Using the Remembered Bible for Building Community,* and *Tell Me the Stories of Jesus: A Companion to the Remembered Gospel* (Wild Goose) and several downloads to use with people of all ages and abilities. She blogs at https://foowr.org.uk/notesfrombambi and you can follow her on Twitter @Bambigoesforth.

Emma Major is a mum, wife, friend, pioneer lay minister, blind wheelchair user and poet. Emma has written a book of poetry about miscarriage and grief and another about mental health. In 2020, her book of poems and pictures about finding hope in loneliness, *Little Guy: Journey of Hope,* was published by Wild Goose. She is a member of the Iona Community. She blogs at http://LLMCalling.blogspot.com

Rebeka Maples is Director of Spiritual Formation for the United Methodist Church programme Course of Study School of Ohio at Methodist Theological School in Ohio. She is retired from parish ministry, after serving churches in England and the U.S. She has a PhD in political science and combines the political and spiritual in her work. She is an associate member of the Iona Community.

John McCall has lived and served in Taiwan for over twenty years. He accompanies seminary students, Asian pastors and the indigenous people of Taiwan. He is an associate of the Iona Community.

Peter Millar is a theologian, campaigner and writer who has worked in many parts of the world, including Iona as Abbey Warden. For the last five years he has lived with an incurable cancer – a journey in which suffering and blessings are interesting companions.

Susan Miller is a member of the Iona Community and a Theology and Religious Studies Tutor at Glasgow University. She has published *Women in Mark's Gospel* (Continuum) and is now working on her next book, *Women in John's Gospel*.

Neil Paynter is an editor, writer and late-night piano player, who lives with his partner Helen, his mum and Stevie the cat in a flat in Biggar, Scotland. Previously he worked in nursing homes and homeless shelters in Canada, London and Scotland. He is an associate of the Iona Community.

Tony Phelan is a member of the Iona Community, a lay preacher and spiritual director. Before he retired, he taught and researched German literature.

Peter Phillips lives in the Cathedral city of Lichfield in the English Midlands. He worked for 26 years as a social worker in Staffordshire, prior to retirement, and was a prison volunteer for eight years. He is a Licensed Reader within the Church of England, and an associate of the Iona Community. In 2017 Peter raised funds for the Iona Abbey Capital Appeal by walking from Lichfield to Iona.

Jan Sutch Pickard is a poet and former Warden in Iona, after which she served with the Ecumenical Accompaniment Programme – both demanding and absorbing tasks in the context of community living. For most of this year she has lived alone in her local community in Mull, sharing with her neighbours the experience of lockdown and uncertainty about the future. Solitude can be a gift for a writer, but – as we all know –

enforced separation from family and friends is hard. So this year has been full of looking outwards, listening, finding creative and new ways to communicate, and often being surprised by the Holy Spirit.

Katharine M Preston is an ecumenical lay preacher and writer, concentrating on issues of social justice and climate change. She is the author of *Field with a View: Science and Faith in a Time of Climate Change* (Wild Goose). Katharine and her husband, John Bingham, live on a farm in Essex, New York and are active associates of the Iona Community.

Bob Rhodes: 'I am a long-term Iona Community associate member and a retired Anglican priest living, with Jill, in Wirksworth, Derbyshire. I look to the Community to help me to maintain my radical edge.'

Jill Rhodes: 'An Iona Community associate for many years and retired counsellor, I enjoy writing poetry and prose, and am glad to have had the opportunity to think about angels in difficult times.'

Catriona Robertson has lived and worked with local communities in the UK, India and the South Pacific. She is a fan of Howard Thurman, who wrote: *'Don't ask what the world needs; ask what brings you alive, because what the world needs is people who have come alive.'* She is Warden of Iona Abbey.

Thom M Shuman, a retired yet still active pastor, has offered morning and evening prayer videos on YouTube during the pandemic. Thom is the author of several books, including *Gobsmacked: Daily Devotions for Advent* (Wild Goose). He is an associate of the Iona Community.

Iain Whyte has been a member of the Iona Community since 1966, and has worked as a University Chaplain, in Church of Scotland parishes, in West Africa and as head of Christian Aid Scotland. He remains active in the areas of Southern Africa and Palestine, and has researched and written on issues of historical and modern racism and slavery.

Isabel Whyte is a member of the Iona Community who first went to an Iona Youth Camp in 1961, then later to cook and lead. She has been a teacher and Healthcare Chaplain and has had a lifelong involvement in peace-making and issues of justice.

Brian Woodcock is a busily retired United Reformed Church minister and ex-Abbey warden, who owes his sanity to his wife and daughters who keep him grounded, to his training in community development, and to his involvement with people and projects within and without the church – where his faith continues to be broadened and tested. He joined the Iona Community for the challenge and support that would keep his ministry on the edge. Questions, rather than answers, energise him and motivate him to energise others.

Martin Wroe is a writer living in London. With Malcolm Doney he is the author of *Lifelines: Notes on Life & Love, Faith & Doubt* (Unbound). He is an associate of the Iona Community.